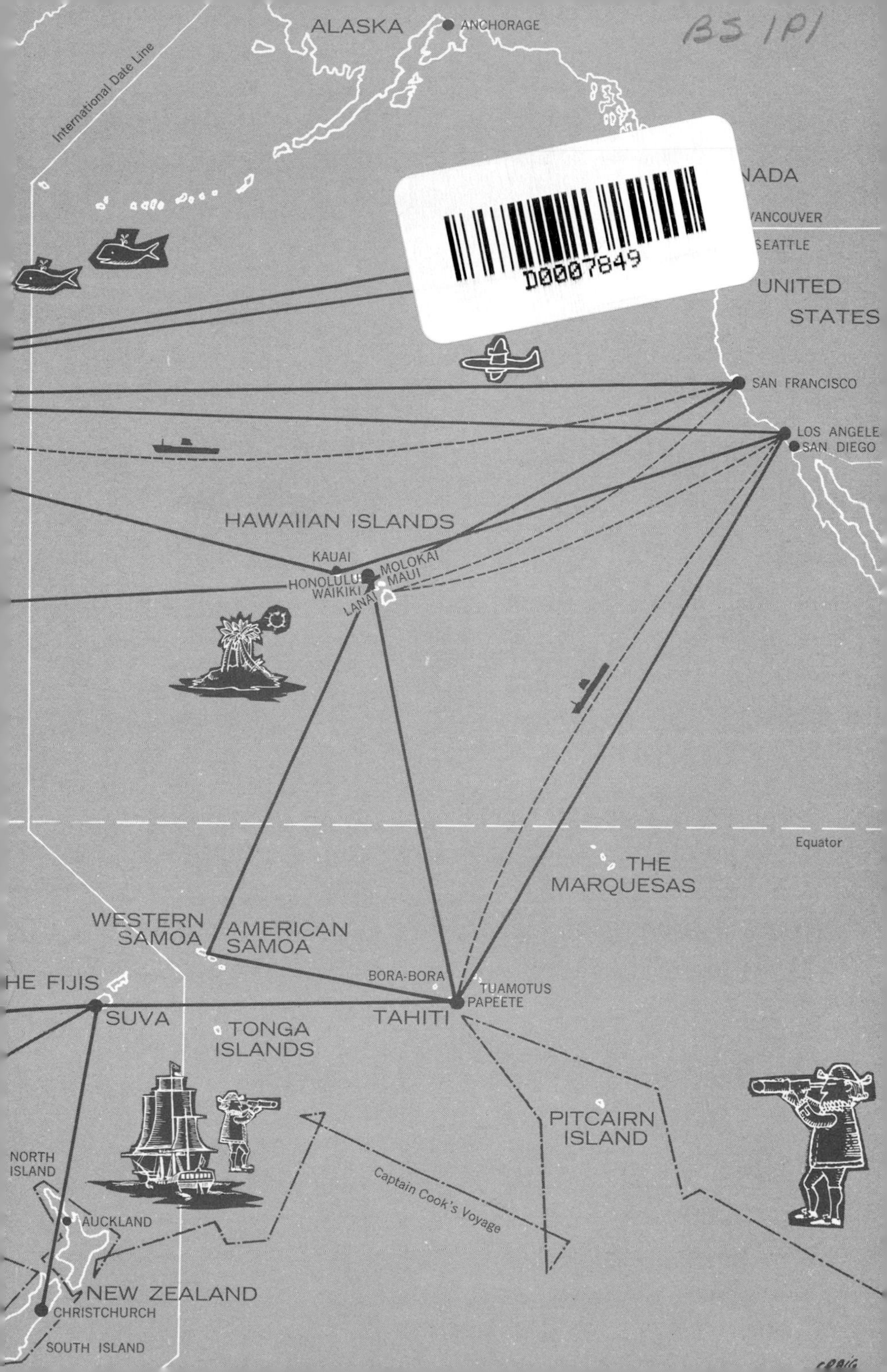
ALASKA
ANCHORAGE
International Date Line
NADA
VANCOUVER
SEATTLE
UNITED
STATES
SAN FRANCISCO
LOS ANGELE
SAN DIEGO
HAWAIIAN ISLANDS
KAUAI
MOLOKAI
HONOLULU
MAUI
WAIKIKI
LANAI
Equator
THE
MARQUESAS
WESTERN
SAMOA
AMERICAN
SAMOA
BORA-BORA
TUAMOTUS
PAPEETE
TAHITI
HE FIJIS
SUVA
TONGA
ISLANDS
PITCAIRN
ISLAND
Captain Cook's Voyage
NORTH
ISLAND
AUCKLAND
NEW ZEALAND
CHRISTCHURCH
SOUTH ISLAND

PACIFIC PATHWAYS

Books by Stan Delaplane

PACIFIC PATHWAYS
POSTCARDS FROM DELAPLANE
THE LITTLE WORLD OF
STANTON DELAPLANE
DELAPLANE IN MEXICO
AND HOW SHE GREW

PACIFIC PATHWAYS

BY STAN DELAPLANE

Illustrated by Richard Rosenblum

McGraw-Hill Book Company

NEW YORK TORONTO LONDON

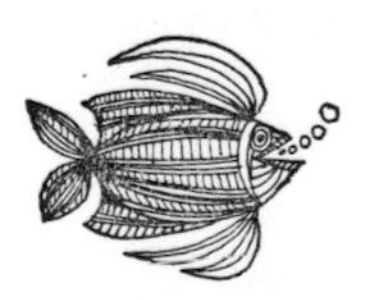

Library of Congress Catalog Card Number: 63-21476

FIRST EDITION

16241

CONTENTS

PREFACE

This is the Pacific, blue and inviting.

Three-fourths of the world's people live on the land basin. Its pathways are traversed by 110-passenger jet liners, 1000-passenger cruise ships, 75-man Polynesian outriggers. By men of good will and men of desperate intent. By gunrunners, missionaries, slave traders, and tourists.

On Pacific lands at this moment, a Chinese scholar is reading 4000-year-old poetry.

A Stone Age man is dying surely of a witchdoctor's curse.

On a lonely island, a forgotten Japanese soldier eats stolen rice, not knowing that World War II is over.

A tribesman in the Philippines prepares to kill and take a head. For manhood and marriage.

In the world's biggest city (Tokyo), the latest dance tunes are playing in the most modern night clubs.

The traveler on Pacific Pathways is well rewarded.

This is not a directory. It is a record of places I've been as a columnist.

If I have not been in some byway, my associate Kevin

Keating has. (He's in Bora Bora so much they keep a ukulele for him there.)

We backed up our own views with experiences of people we know, whose tastes we agree with—foreign correspondents, airline men, residents we met in these places.

If you go as far as Japan ($783 round-trip from the West Coast of America), I advise you to pay $417 more for the round-the-Pacific fare. It gives you 17 major cities from Tokyo down to Sydney and to Auckland and home through the South Pacific. It's a travel buy and you can alternate between ship and plane.

The Pacific is changing. Travel is increasing. This book is not meant to do all your exploring for you. It will get you started and keep you charted.

PACIFIC PATHWAYS

HAWAII

"Go for broke!"

The shell horn blowing early for examination of the schools, in the meeting house. About 2000 scholars present, some wrapped in large quantity of native cloth, with wreaths of evergreen about their heads and hanging toward their feet —others dressed in calico and silk with large necklaces of braided hair and wreaths of yellow and green feathers very beautiful and expensive.

It was a pleasant occasion, in which they seemed interested and happy. The king and chiefs were present, and examined among the rest. They read in various books, and 450 in four rows wrote the same sentence at the same time on slate.

They perform with some ceremony. In this exercise, one of the teachers cried out with as much importance as an orderly sergeant . . . and immediately the whole company began to sit up straight. At the next order they stood on their feet. At the next they "handled" slates or "presented"— i.e. they held them resting on the left arm as a musician would place his fiddle. At the next order they brought their pencils to bear upon the broadsides of their slates ready for action. Mr. Bingham then put into the crier's ear the sentence to be written, which he proclaimed with all his might and a movement of the 450 pencils commenced which from their creaking was like the music of machinery lacking oil.

—from the diary of missionary the Rev. Reuben Tinker; description of an examination that took place in Honolulu in 1831

MONEY. U.S. dollar (the more the merrier)

BEST TIME TO GO. Anytime. Year-round trade-winds climate.

LANGUAGE. The Oceanic speech family can be traced to Malaysia. It runs through thousands of miles of ocean, through high islands and atolls. In spite of the *Kon-tiki* raft experiment, language students find no trace of American Indian.

Visitors pick up a little Polynesian for color.

While language has split (somewhat like the differences between Italian, Spanish, and French), there are words that sound alike: Hawaiians say *hale* for house, Tahitians say *fale,* Samoans say *fare.*

Cook Islanders and New Zealand Maoris seem to understand each other completely, the last migration dating back less than 2000 years.

The language shows the effects of travel through Micronesia and Melanesia.

It has 10 to 14 consonants and depends on vowel repetition. There's fish shorter than its name: *humuhumunukunukuuapuaa.*

All of the islands have picked up the language of the present owners:

Hawaii is a mixture of English, English-pidgin, Japanese and Chinese and Polynesian: "Whassamatta you, you no stop? I t'ink you catch too much *wahine pilikia.*"

In every group of islands there is one called *Hawaii, Havaki* or something similar. The name refers to the original birthplace of the race, supposedly in Malaysia or India.

You pick up the local words for thank you and hello without trouble.

Hawaiian is most fun.

The newest state, Hawaii, entertains 350,000 tourists

a year. Under skies as blue as a Chinaman's pants. Caressed by trade winds as silken as a Japanese kimono.

There are five lush islands. But the tourists insist on jamming into some 10 blocks along Waikiki.

This has created skyscraper hotels. Overlapping bathers in the 70-degree surf. Parking problems and other irritants by which we destroy ourselves with such gusto. (In the last 10 years, aloha-shirt shops have swallowed up the tropical gardens at the Royal Hawaiian. And the manager of the Hilton Hawaiian Village plans to build a 27-floor hotel on the parking lot. "At these land prices, I can't let it stand empty.")

Even so, there is a warm, tropical feeling of Pacific Islands. (Rare is the girl who doesn't tuck a hibiscus blossom in her hair. Rare is the man who doesn't sigh like a breaker at the sight of all that coconut cream pie tanning on the beach.)

There is a bustle of business about Waikiki these days.

But the daily parade of muumuus, the leisurely lei-sellers threading fragrant *pikake,* the soft hiss of water washing on the white sand—all make this one of the wondrous vacation places of the world.

The finest thing about Hawaii is the price. A six-day vacation, hotel included, from the West Coast starts at about $280.

You arrive by ship at Aloha Tower. By air at Honolulu Airport. Therefore no formalities from the U.S.—this *is* the United States.

No health problems. Not even a mosquito. The only hazards here are sunburn and overeating.

Somebody will drop a flower lei about your neck on landing. The custom is to kiss you on the cheek on presenting a lei. If you buy a lei for your wife in the

evening, be sure to put it on her and give her a quick smooch.

While the language is English, everybody drops a dash of Hawaiian into the talk.

Malihini is a newcomer. *Kamaaina* is an old-timer. (They used to have special rates at the hotels for islanders. Known as *kamaaina* rates.)

A woman is a *wahine*. *Pilikia* is trouble. You no give your wahine a lei and smooch each evening, you get much wahine pilikia.

The currency is American. Airmail to the mainland is just like it is from New York to San Francisco—and just as fast.

Boy meets girl. Like falling off a coconut log. Waikiki Beach is a garden of unattached males and females. I suggest:

The lanai (terrace) of the Moana Hotel at sunset.

The circular garden bar near the beach at the Hilton Hawaiian Village.

Around the pool at the Princess Kaiulani.

Send the lady a *mai tai*, a rummy concoction with a stick of pineapple in it. They go for $1.50 a smash. But they blow in your veins like a conch shell.

Tipping is just like home. About 15 per cent on the restaurant bill. A quarter for the bellboy. In addition, when you leave, send a couple of dollars to the beach boy—the Hawaiian who handed you your towels.

The beach boys are the only 100-per-cent Hawaiians. A little caste system of the plush and private Outrigger Club which is open only to pure Hawaiians or pure sugar aristocracy.

All the rest of the hotel help is a mixture or descendants of Japanese, Chinese and Filipinos, the workmen who built the Islands.

It has made a beautiful people. The Polynesian that was stirred in keeps everybody a little on the slow-down side. That and the sun and surf and a soft climate it's a shame to work in.

Visitors get what is called Polynesian paralysis:

"You lie down and can't get up again."

* * *

Dress is very informal. I wear khaki slacks and an aloha shirt—those sport shirts worn outside the pants.

These used to be a flaming pattern of all-colored pineapples.

Today the aloha shirt has calmed down. A small pattern over the shirt pocket is considered OK. Andrade's on Kalakaua Boulevard, the main street, is excellent. (Also their shop in the Royal Hawaiian.)

McInerney's is very good. I also like Ross Sutherland's shops in the hotels and on the boulevard.

For women, I like Carol and Mary shops in the hotels. The muumuu, the Mother Hubbard introduced by the missionaries in 1820, has been updated.

You get them short. You get them long. You get them with a Chinese collar (when it is called a *pake-muu, pake* being the Hawaiian word for Chinese).

It is cool. It fits the climate. You can wear it day and night. It is colorful. Get one immediately.

There is some dressing for dinner. I mean coat-and-tie kind of dressing. At Canlis Broiler, one of the best restaurants. In the main dining room of the Royal Hawaiian and in the Makahiki Room of the Hawaiian Village.

Bring a minimum of clothes. Buy what you need here.

The selection is better. The price is better.

The variety of bathing suits is fantastic. No matter what you bring, you'll want to buy something here.

It doesn't rain enough to bother you. I've never carried an umbrella or raincoat in Hawaii.

It's never cool enough to wear a topcoat.

Nylon watchbands are cooler and are always better for men in the tropics. Leather watchbands go to pieces.

Women need a few cocktail dresses. And a man will find places where he can wear a dinner jacket (though it's not necessary). Make it tropical weight.

* * *

Downtown Honolulu is not inspiring. A standard American city of 231,000 people.

There are a couple of night clubs, mostly importing Japanese floor shows from the Nichigeiki Theater in Tokyo.

The action is around Waikiki. I've found good:

All day around the circular, outside bar at the Hilton Hawaiian Village. Free hula lessons in the morning. A performance you *must* see.

Roast-pig ceremony certain days at noon. Hawaiian boys carrying the pig. The leader blowing ceremonial notes on a conch shell. They roast the pig in an underground oven called an *imu.* (The clicking of cameras sounds like a thousand grasshoppers taking off.)

An orchestra and dancing at night.

There's also a more dressy show and dinner in the main dining room.

Royal Hawaiian Hotel: Very pretty lanai bar beside the beach. (I don't like the music. It's been organ stuff.) Good drinks. Good service.

A *mai tai* beside the beach at the older, quieter Halekulani. Hawaiian music and some nice hula. Good *hors d'oeuvres* called here *pupus*.

Beside the pool at the Princess Kaiulani. Hawaiian music. Good drinks. Nice atmosphere. Nice bar inside with Philippine-style breezeways.

The lanai beside the big banyan tree in the courtyard of the Moana, oldest of the beach hotels. Hawaiian music and a lot of surf coming up beside you.

For dinner:

The Tahitian Lanai. One of Spence Weaver's restaurants. Tahitian bar with black velvet paintings and a bartender in a red pompon French sailor hat serving the drinks. The waitresses wear the flowery head lei instead of the Hawaiian lei that goes around the neck.

Excellent Pacific lobster. And you can get the Tahitian raw-fish-in-lime cocktail here. You eat under a thatched roof beside the sea with candlelight.

Canlis Broiler. Owned by Pete Canlis and run by Lloyd Samaha. The ladies' powder room is a show spot of the islands. So good that they run the *wahines* out of it once in a while and give the gentlemen a peek at the decor. (The famous ladies' Pearl Room at the Royal Hawaiian is another one that sends the ladies out raving.)

Waitresses are Japanese in kimonos. Steaks the best in the Islands. (Meat in the early days was a seldom,

unrefrigerated thing in Hawaii. So Catholics have a special dispensation to eat meat on Friday here.)

You should have reservations. In the upper dining room, you must wear coat and tie.

The Royal Hawaiian. One of the best in Hawaii. A good, Hawaiian-style floor show with plenty of hula. Dancing on the lanai.

* * *

Lot of little places along Kalakaua Boulevard with good food. Inexpensive. Plenty of Chinese and Japanese places. Real Hawaiian food is unexciting–roast pig and *poi,* a sort of paste that you have to be raised on to like.

Most food you get will have the Pacific flavor of Japan and China behind all those Hawaiian names on the menu.

* * *

The International Market Place off the boulevard is full of small shops with Pacific wares: planters' straw hats, shell necklaces, Hong Kong ivory, Japanese slippers.

They also have a number of little snack bars with Japanese or Chinese cooking. Good for lunch.

The Barefoot Bar at Queen's Surf has a lot of music

and a good monologue-singing show by Sterling Mossman and a Hawaiian combo.

Don the Beachcomber's is now called Duke Kahanamoku's—he's the ex-sheriff and old-time swimmer. It's good.

Speaking of the barefoot life: Try dancing barefoot here. You'll like it. Gives you that happy island feeling.

Hilton opens a new luxury hotel—the Kahala—in December 1963. On the grounds of Waialae Country Club.

The Outer Islands

Not as lively as Waikiki but a quiet charm all their own. Every hotel has a travel desk selling a tour of the outer islands. It's inexpensive and takes about five days. Aloha Airlines and Hawaiian Airlines fly it.

HAWAII

Known as the Big Island. You land on the Kona coast. Best hotels are the Kona Inn and Gus Guslander's new King Kamehameha.

Food is good. Nice drives. Good swimming. Entertainment at cocktails and after dinner.

There is a booming real estate drive on this lava flow. Everybody's selling lots a mile from nowhere. But who knows.... They used to laugh at people who bought lots in Hollywood, it was so far from Los Angeles.

MAUI

One of the Hawaiian kings (encouraged by missionaries) once sent erring subjects here for punishment. It was a new law about Boy Meeting Girl without benefit of New England clergy.

The convicted Hawaiians built the Maui roads. You will be glad to know as you sightsee that you are riding on a primrose path.

Hana Maui is the elegant hotel here. The Sheraton Maui is the newest. The older Maui Palms is now operated by a *hui* of Honolulu Hawaiian-Japanese. I haven't been there since they took over. Was inexpensive and good.

KAUAI

The Garden Island, 30 flying minutes from Honolulu. Hanalei Plantation House overlooks the valley and the long, white beach where they filmed *South Pacific*. This is a Guslander operation. Very plush. Everybody has his own cottage, view, and a little cable-car ride down the hill to the beach.

Coco Palms is in a grove of coco palms alongside what used to be the royal fishponds.

The tours usually give you an overnight here. You sleep in a bed made of an outrigger canoe. Bathe in an outside rock bath all your own. Entertainment every night. Much blowing of conch shells and a bunch of Hawaiian boys run through the trees lighting luau torches.

The islands of **Molokai** (the leper-colony island) and **Lanai** are still in development stage. There are hotels if you are doing a leisurely exploration. Not for tourists generally.

* * *

For the adventurous there's some wild-pig hunting on the Big Island. The local boys grab them by the throat and stick them with a knife. Some wild-goat shooting and you can do some horseback riding—there's a big cattle operation on the island.

Honolulu Hotels

Royal Hawaiian. Best known, second oldest in the Islands. The big pink building is on the widest part of wide Waikiki Beach. Lobby is high and airy. Plush carpets and lots of marble. The lobby is dressy. It's the only place in the Islands where a woman can get away with a long evening dress. Quiet—except for the beach. The food is good, the shops are expensive, and the Hawaiian show in the Monarch Room is first-class. I like to sit on the open-air lanai and watch the activity on the beach. The mynah birds drink with you. Expensive.

Hawaiian Village. The lively spot these sunny days. Lots of young people. The hotel is huge and rambling. Chrome and glass and air conditioning make for a lively, antiseptic paradise. The beach isn't as good as the main part of Waikiki. There are five pools. And too much going on—hula lessons, swimming lessons, ukulele lessons. Dancing, catamaran trips, surfing. The works. It's a little far from central Waikiki. A six-to-nine-block walk. Hotel entertainment is good. (The Shell Bar was made by TV's *Hawaiian Eye.*) And there is

nightly dancing under the stars at the Garden Bar and dining in the Makahiki Room. Moderate to expensive.

Moana. The radio show *Hawaii Calls* originated here. (Now alternates between the Moana, the Hawaiian Village, and the Reef.) The oldest hotel. And the quietest—except on the *makai* side (toward the water), where they hose down the courtyard under the big banyan tree at 5:30 every morning. Much scraping of chairs. And if the *mai tais* knocked your coconut hat into the lagoon the night before, you won't like it. Moderate to expensive.

Princess Kaiulani. Good all round. (Except for the restaurant on the corner.) Well located, prices are reasonable, and the Diamond Head wing is air-conditioned. The rooms are small but well decorated. Nice piano bar.

Surfrider. Connected to Moana. Small rooms, moderate to expensive. Good restaurant off the lobby. Captain Cook Room.

Halekulani. Visitors who return year after year like this one. It's quiet and right on the beach. Nice for Sunday-morning breakfasts.

The Reef. Right next door to the Halekulani. Unfortunately, when you book there is no guarantee you'll get a room *mauka, makai,* or Diamond Head. But avoid one Ewa side or you've had it. The new YMCA building seems less than a foot away.

Tropic Isle. If you're on a budget. Ask for John Gorbett. Central, at Waikiki about a block and a half from the beach.

Hotel rooms are nearly always available all year round. But I'd recommend you reserve. Hawaii Hotel Association will help you if you run into trouble. Small hotels with kitchens and apartment hotels are available by the day, week and month.

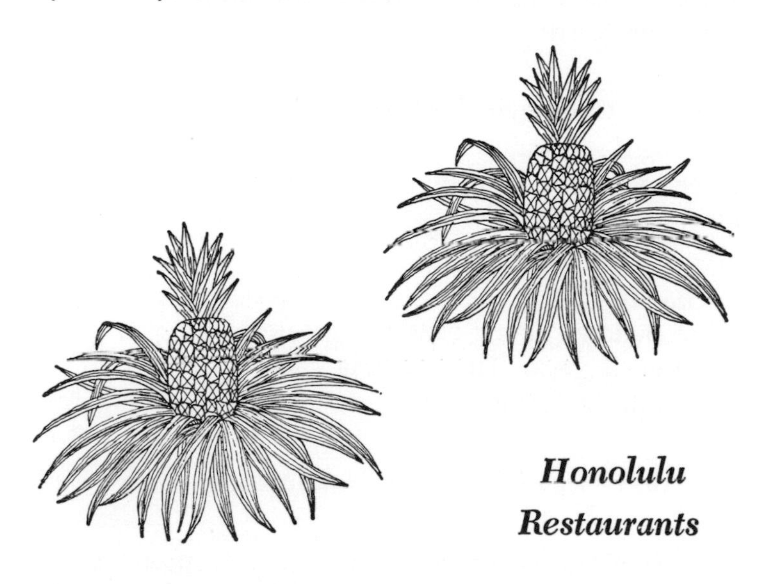

Honolulu Restaurants

Canlis Charcoal Broiler. I'm partial to this restaurant. I like Peter Canlis and I like the food he serves. Excellent piano bar. Try his special salad. He'll insist on showing you his newly decorated ladies' room. He's very proud of the gold dolphin faucet handles. Lloyd Samaha's your host when Peter isn't around.

Tahitian Lanai. Excellent for *mahi mahi.* And be sure to check the bar for the original Leeteg paintings from Tahiti. They're on black velvet.

Michels. Many Islanders think this is the best of all. In the lobby of the Colony Surf Co-op out Diamond

Head way. Go about sunset and watch the *tiki*-torches being fired out on the water. Piano bar.

Tropics. Good for lunch or dinner. A big spot for the Waikiki business lunch. African safari trophies all over the walls. Terrific roast beef.

Gourmet. Good roast beef on Kalakaua Boulevard. Refreshing if you want a change from tropical decor. Good place for fun in the evenings. Spence Weaver runs this now.

La Ronde. This is the spinner on top of the Ala Moana office building. Food isn't the greatest, but you get a sensational view. The revolving motion seems to go away after a martini or two.

Ishii Gardens. I like this one for Japanese food.

Lau Yee Chai. Islanders kid this place by pronouncing it Lousy Chow. The decor is outstanding in the Chinese fashion. The food is OK but it ain't Hong Kong.

Pat's at Punaluu. Halfway round the Island. Many people drive from Honolulu just for lunch, it's that good.

Waioli Tea Room. Nearly all tours stop here for lunch. But if you miss it, run over on your own. It's in the Manoa section of town. And I think the prettiest. Great gardens, lawns, wooded areas. Run by the Salvation Army home for girls. The girls do all the cooking and serving. Recipes date from missionary days. Before you eat, the girls collect in the dining room and sing the Doxology in Hawaiian. Grass shacks on the grounds and a lava-rock chapel. Closed Sundays and Mondays.

Wisteria. Another good place for Japanese cooking. And Hawaiian. *Lau lau, poi, lomi lomi* salmon, everything. Between Waikiki and downtown Honolulu.

Jo Jans. Plush. Moderate to expensive menu. Very good food. Piano bar and a splashing colored fountain. Favored by locals with *kalaa* ($$$).

Night Clubs and Entertainment

Barefoot Bar. Sterling Mossman, a former police detective, is the highlight here. Complete Polynesian review. Spence Weaver runs the place. He owns the Hotel Tahiti in Papeete and gets first crack at Tahitian entertainers.

Duke Kahanamoku's. In the International Market Place. This used to be Don the Beachcomber's, and since the change they've jazzed up the show and the decor. It's touristy and good.

Na Kupuna Night. Every Wednesday night at the Moana Banyan Courtyard. *Na Kupuna* means "old-timer," and the entertainment is Gay '90s, Hawaiian style.

Night in Japan. Every Friday at the Princess Kaiulani hotel. Just what it says.

Tapa Room, Hawaiian Village. Expensive. Good Hawaiian show, sometimes entertainers from the Mainland.

Monarch Room, Royal Hotel. Firstest of the first-class shows.

Luaus. Plenty of camera-snapping at these hoked-up versions of how the Polynesian feast operates. But you've got to see one. Most hotels have their own. I think the Queen's Surf does it best. The *puaa* goes in the *imu* (pig in the oven) about one in the afternoon, and cooks on the hot lava rocks for about six hours.

Plenty of other places to go. Check the papers, the *Waikiki Beach Press,* and local entertainment guides. Or call the Hawaii Visitor's Bureau at 92-211.

Shopping

Good shops all over Waikiki. Wait until you arrive for buying clothes. Better selection than you can get at home. And a lot more comfortable and colorful. Ladies just *have* to have a muumuu. And don't belt it! Polished cottons are big these fashionable days. Chinese art objects are good buys. Wood carvings and monkey-pod wood dishes. (Check the little shop next to the

Liberty House store.) Black velvet paintings, black coral jewelry, sun hats.

Watamull Shops. Good for all kinds of Hawaiian wear, Indian textiles, etc.

Ross Sutherland. Men's beach and sports wear. Good selection of sport shirts. Many, many shops. Too many to list. I also liked **Andrades, Liberty House, McInerney's, Carol and Mary's.** And many of the shops in the International Market Place.

Tours may be selected for you when you arrive. But if you book your own, choose a small tour company. The larger ones treat you as part of the herd.

Tape Tours is a new and interesting way to get around. You rent a car equipped with a tape recorder. You're given a map with places of interest marked. When you come to a marked location, stop the car and turn on the tape. All the information you want is prerecorded. And you can take all the time you want all around the island.

TO READ ON THE WAY. Michener's *Hawaii,* Bob Krauss' *Travel Guide to the Hawaiian Islands, Last King of Paradise* by Eugene Burns, Mary Pukui's *Legends of the Islands of Hawaii.*

FOR MORE INFORMATION. Hawaii Visitor's Bureau, 2051 Kalakaua Avenue—also offices in New York, Chicago, San Francisco, and Los Angeles. Check the phone book. Pacific Area Travel Association, 442 Post Street, San Francisco. And your carrier.

HOW TO GET THERE

Airlines: Pan American and United Airlines fly from the West Coast several times daily, the only U.S. airlines permitted to terminate passengers in the Islands. All other major Pacific lines may allow passengers to stop over en route to further points.

Inside the Islands, you fly Aloha or Hawaiian Airlines —both excellent, with convenient schedules.

Steamship Lines: American President Lines, Matson Navigation Company, P & O–Orient Lines, Pacific Far East Lines.

Outer Island Hotels

HAWAII

Volcano House. Is 32 miles from Hilo, on the edge of Kilauea crater in Hawaii National Park. Golf course one mile away. Tours through the park and around the craters. Languages spoken are Spanish, Japanese, German, and Italian as well as English and pidgin.

KONA COAST

Kona Inn. Hawaiian entertainment nightly. And all the activity you want. Swimming pool, ocean bathing, tennis, deep-sea fishing, croquet, badminton, shuffleboard, skindiving, volleyball, and catamaran rides available.

King Kamehameha. About the same size (105 rooms) as the Kona Inn, with dancing and entertainment. Glass-bottom boat, too.

HILO

Hilo. Air conditioning, but they charge $1 extra to turn it on. A show three evenings a week. Piano other evenings. Golf courses four and six miles away. Swimming pool.

Hilo Hukilau. On Kuhio Bay, with a pool if you prefer fresh water.

Naniloa. European or American plan. Add $8 for American plan. Golf, croquet. Swimming pool.

KAUAI—HANALEI BAY

Hanalei Plantation. Bali H'ai luxury. Every sport including wild-pig hunting and billiards. Seven miles from town; you really can get away from the racket here. The greatest.

KAUAI—KOLOA AND POIPU BEACH VICINITY

Prince Kuhio. Apartments with kitchenettes available, as well as rooms.

Waiohai. Suitelike rooms on an excellent beach. Lanais and bath, fresh and salt-water pools. Expensive.

KAUAI—LIHUE AND KAPAA VICINITY

Coco Palms. Another Guslander hotel, with 145 rooms and lots to do, or as much as you can find anywhere on the Garden Island.

Kauai Surf. Golf, pool. Japanese, Korean, Chinese, Filipino, and Spanish spoken.

Kauai Inn. Owned by the same troops as the Kauai Surf. Limousines shuttle between the two hotels. Guests have privileges of both.

MAUI

Hotel Hana-Maui. All the activities plus a 15-horse stable.

Maui Palms Hotel. On the bayshore, with a surrounding mountain view.

Old Whaler's Pioneer Inn. They're building 80 new rooms here. With showers.

Sheraton Maui. Four miles from Lahaina. On the famous Black Rock promontory, in a garden setting. On the ocean. The newest.

LANAI

The island is mostly pineapple plantation. One hotel, the **Lanai Inn,** at 1600 feet in the pine trees. Moderate.

MOLOKAI

This is building up a little bit. But not much tourist attraction yet. The **Molokai Seaside Inn** is about it. Moderate rates for 20 cottage-type and bungalow rooms with private baths. Tours are conducted to the old leper colony.

Tours

I think Hawaii looks best from the lanai of the Halekulani on Waikiki Beach or from the hilltop at Hanalei Plantation House on Kauai—with a big, frosty *mai tai* in hand.

I rode around an awful lot of island looking at pineapple and sugar cane—all of which look good for a couple of miles but not for five islands' worth.

What I mean is that there are places to see. But don't let them drive you through a hundred miles of sugar cane to get there.

Everybody goes and should go—

Around-the-Island Tour ($8–$10 for one day; pay your own lunch)

This takes you on a circular tour around Oahu. Bus is cheapest. Car is a little more but you have more freedom. They always stop at the Blowhole, for instance. And unless you think it is splendid to see sea water spout out of sea rocks, it gets tiresome. The photographers on your bus can take a half-hour just waiting for the right jet of water.

The pineapple cannery is on this run.

Chinatown has the best flavor this side of Hong Kong.

Monkeypod furniture manufacturing is interesting. (Prices pretty high.)

You see the Buddhist church, royal mausoleum, Oahu Country Club, Upside Down Falls, coral factories. An imposing Mormon Temple—a lot of Samoans live in this area. Samoans are the best thatch-weavers in the South Pacific. These people make a living thatching the little grass-shack cocktail lounges of Waikiki.

This is a long sugar-cane drive. Eventually you come to Schofield Barracks and return through the shoreline drive past Pearl Harbor.

Mount Tantalus and City of Honolulu (about $7)

Less sugar cane and a little more rewarding in my opinion. Here's the list of sights usually pointed out on this standard tour: the Shriner's hospital and grounds—Mormon Temple—Washington Place, residence of the Governor and the old mansion of Hawaiian kings—City Hall—Library—Iolani Palace, royalty's only residence in the U.S.—Kamehameha's statue—Civic Center

—Punchbowl Crater, now the site of the Pacific War Memorial Cemetery—a view of Honolulu from the top of Mount Tantalus—Punahou School, founded by the missionaries in 1841—and usually a stop at the Waioli Tea Room for lunch. (You buy your own. It's not usually included on the tour.)

Diamond Head, Koko Head, Kailua (about $7)
This takes you about 50 miles along the coast. You'll see Kapiolani Park, Diamond Head, and the residential areas (including Doris Duke's mansion). Koko Crater and Kokohead Park. Hanauma Bay. The Blowhole, the most photographed thing in Honolulu after the luau. Makapuu lighthouse, the strongest in the world. And back over the Pali with a spectacular view of the windward coast. This is where King Kamehameha pushed over the opposing warriors and united the Islands. Some say 10,000. Some say 1000. Some say less than 300.

Some say the King didn't push them over the Pali. They backed off and fell over in surprise when he suggested they quit eating *poi.*

Pearl Harbor Cruise ($7 to $10)
Definitely worthwhile. About 3½ hours on a power boat or catamaran visiting the naval shipyard and drydocks, the Naval Air Station and Ford Island, scenes of the December 7 attack, plus a visit to Battleship Row where the *Utah* and *Arizona* are sunk. Well done, informative, and a pleasant boat ride.

General Tours
The **Night Club Tour** usually hits a Japanese show (imported), a table at the Royal Hawaiian, and one of the more Polynesian-type places. A drink in each. $12–$15. **Luau parties** are a must-do. Sit around *ti*-leaf-covered tables and eat pig out of the underground oven. Try a

little *poi.* Hula dancing. Ukuleles. And leis and island atmosphere. About $10.

Hukilau tour, or fishing party. About $4, with additional transportation charge of about $4.

Big-game fishing goes for about $50 on the half-day charter, $85 for a full day.

A **catamaran cruise** of one hour to Diamond Head goes right off Waikiki Beach between Moana and the Royal Hawaiian. $3.50.

Much better—I do this one regularly—is the **sunset supper ride** from the Hawaiian Village. $9.50 for cocktails and dinner with plenty of sunset and music.

And there's a sailing-schooner ride on the barkentine *California.* Dinner and trip for $9.95. Very pleasant.

There are **glass-bottom-boat tours** for $2.50. Every hotel lobby has a tour desk selling all of these trips. They are standard and good. Children are usually half-price.

If you're in one of the smaller hotels off the beach with no tour desk, the main street of Waikiki—Kalakaua Boulevard—is stiff with agents who will sell you anything. Prices are competitive and don't vary much.

A **walking tour** you can take on your own: through the International Market Place on Kalakaua Boulevard.

Free Industry Tours

Your hotel desk can give you hours for these. You can go through pineapple canneries, sugar mills, a perfume factory, a tuna-packing plant, a brewery, and a woodworking factory. All for free.

Outer Island Tours (Cost varies according to time and transportation)

The better islands to visit are Kauai (my first choice—half-hour from Honolulu), Hawaii (the Big Island), and Maui.

Kauai Tour ($13–$20 for one to two days)
Gives you a trip up the Wailua River by boat—Captain Cook made his first contact with the Hawaiian Islands offshore here. A visit to Hanapepe, a typical plantation town. A trip to Waimea Canyon, a spectacular sight. Seaside ride to Hanalei, where *South Pacific* was filmed.

Kauai's great attraction to me is the small plantation towns and the feeling that it has been lightly touched by the tourist invasion.

Big Island Tours (Cost varies through 19 different tour patterns)
For $11–$18 you can take one-day tours that visit the town of Hilo, the Volcanoes National Park, Kona on the beautiful lava coast, the Parker ranch.

For $23.84 you make a day and a half of the same with a little history thrown in. Captain Cook was killed here.

For $28.30–$31.70 there are three-day "round-the-island" tours. This usually includes 3½ hours on the *Coral Queen,* which cruises by the Cook Monument and remains of native temples.

Maui Tours ($11.35 for one day, $16.75 for two)
Lot of sugar-cane driving but you do get to see the original whaler-missionary port of Lahaina, suddenly coming to life again with the new Sheraton hotel nearby.

Various sailor ports competed for the title "Hellhole of the Pacific." Lahaina was one. Current developers are raising cocktail parlors to the status—or perhaps the reconstruction—of sailor dens.

They have the feeling of most reconstructions—they may look the same but it's a different crowd doing it.

There's a pretty drive up to Mount Haleakala and the coastal drive is of interest.

All these tours can be booked in Honolulu, or at home through a travel agent.

The flights by Aloha or Hawaiian Airlines are short. So short that now, since they are putting in jets, Hawaiian Air figures no flight will be more than 12 minutes from "seat belts off" to "seat belts on" again.

They're wondering what the stewardesses can serve in 12 minutes.

For old Hawaii, you can visit Molokai, still undeveloped but with hotel accommodations. You find pretty much a fish-and-*poi* life in the villages.

You have to ask for it. Not included on most tours.

AND ANOTHER THING

Naturally, you'll do a breaker ride in the outrigger canoes—$1.50 a ride.

But you might miss a sunset catamaran cruise with cocktails and music. One of those things that makes you sing "Some Enchanted Evening" and puts an aloha lump in your throat. Leave evenings from the Hilton Hawaiian Village.

* * *

If you depart for the Mainland by boat, throw your lei in the water off Waikiki. If it floats back to shore, you'll come back to Hawaii. If it's a particularly expensive lei—maunaloa orchid—one of the coin-diving boys following your boat will fish it out and *take* it ashore. (They dry them out and sell them again.)

* * *

Go for broke is Hawaiian for "shoot the works." It was the motto of the highly decorated Hawaiian-Japanese 442nd Regimental Combat Team.

JAPAN

"Catchee Japanese wife,
Chinese cook,
***American paycheck.* Ichi ban.**
Number One!"

It seems to me that in this country they act with honor and obedience rather because they think they would lose their honour if they acted contrarily, than of fear of the punishment they would receive if disobedient. They are small eaters, albeit heavy drinkers, and they drink rice wine since there are no ordinary wines in these parts. They are men who never gamble, because they consider it a great dishonor, since those who gamble desire what is not theirs and hence tend to become thieves. They swear but little, and when they do it is by the Sun. There are many persons who can read and write, which is a great help to their learning quickly prayers and religious matters. It is a land where there are but few thieves in some kingdoms, and this is by the strict justice which is executed against those who are, for their lives are never spared. They abhor beyond measure the vice of theft. They are a people of good will, very sociable and very desirous of knowledge; they are very fond of hearing things of God, chiefly when they understand them. Of all the lands which I have seen in my life, whether those of Christians or of heathens, never yet did I see a people so honest in not thieving. I discovered fewer sins in the laity and found them more obedient to reason, than those whom they regard as fathers and priests, whom they call Bonzes.

—part of a letter from
Francis Xavier, S.J., to the
Jesuits at Goa; dated Kagoshima,
November 5, 1549

MONEY. 360 Japanese yen to $1 U.S.
BEST TIME TO GO. April–May, October–November
LANGUAGE. Rich in apologies for even being alive. The language is so polite that the Japanese will apologize twice in a sentence that contains no more than good wishes for the morning.

"Pardon me," "I am offending you," "I am so sorry" are larded into a sentence like "Shall I serve you peaches with your breakfast?"

The language is hard to learn. Verbs take many different forms to express what and how the noun is doing.

There is some humor in it. But smiling or laughing is hidden by the palm of the hand. It's impolite to show the teeth.

A sentence is spoken with a final indrawn hiss—to prevent offense if the speaker hasn't used his chlorophyll pills today.

Visitors learn a few phrases: Thank you—*domo arigato;* please—*dozo* to be used in "please come in" to the maid: you're welcome—*doy tashimashtai.*

People in names or address should be followed with *san* in place of "Mr., Mrs. or Miss." I am "Derraprane-san" at the Press Club. The boy who pages me is "Boy-san." So is a cocktail waitress "Boy-san." But a maid is "Girl-san," or, if her name is Yuki, for example, "Yuki-san."

Famous people merit the prefix O. Kichi, the alleged girl friend of the first American ambassador, becomes "O-Kichi." The *O* is "honorable." However, Sacred Mount Fuji (you see Japanese on the roads dismount and bow to it) is known as Fuji-san. Why it isn't O-Fuji I don't know.

The entry to the hotel goes like this:

The maid meets you on her knees. She bows so that her head almost touches the floor.

"Good morning, Derraprane-san excuse me. Here are

your honorable slippers I am offending you. Your room is down the hall I beg your pardon."

Things become honorable, too.

Chopsticks are *hashi*. But you ask for the *o-hashi*. Tea is *cha*. You ask for *o-cha*. Even the humble rice roll, *sushi*, is *o-sushi*. Excuse me, pardon me, I am offending you. *Domo arigato.*

Japanese girls have an endearing custom: They light *your* cigarettes. That puts Japan 10 points up right now.

By air, you land at modern Haneda Airport. By sea probably at Yokohama.

You can bring 200 cigarettes or 50 cigars and five fifths of whisky, which is costly in Japan. Ask for the special tax-free certificate when you pass through Customs, and show it when you buy things.

City-type dressing. You'll want a dark suit for evening and cocktail dresses for the ladies. Suits on the streets in the daytime. You could bring sport shirts and dresses for the country. But you probably won't need them.

The Japanese inns issue you daily a kimono thing called a *yukata*.

Most Japanese wear these right out on the street in the hot-springs resorts. It takes a little nerve the first time. After that you'll love it.

The *yukata*, by the way, is a walking Diners' Club card.

Your hotel name is on your sleeve. Most stores will look at this and charge to your hotel.

(You have no pants, see? So how are you going to carry money?)

Tokyo has become an expensive town. The prices are beginning to match those of New York and Paris.

No health problems. You can drink the water. Japanese doctors and dentists are excellent.

No prescriptions needed. You can go into any drugstore and buy anything you want. And I'd certainly take a look at the American Drug Store in the Nikkatsu Building—just to see chain grocery-store sales methods applied to remedies for tired blood.

There are several "sex stores" dealing in amazing things that the Japanese feel are so specialized they belong in special establishments. You'll find them listed in the classified sections of the English-language *Nippon Times* or *Asahi Evening News.*

There are a few health-food restaurants. They specialize in such things as raw snake *sashimi*—which, as anyone knows, keeps you young. Big hangout for the theatrical crowd.

* * *

You'll probably stay at the famous Imperial. The luxurious Okura. The Nikkatsu. The newer New Japan. Or the smaller, cheaper Dai Ichi. The Akasaka Prince is a little farther from the shopping districts but is more Japanese.

The Tokyo Hilton is for people who dig Conrad's special touch: The do-it-yourself dial system. The tuck-away beds and Oriental touches on top of the Hilton system, which is standard and reliable all over the world.

It's hard to find top-grade Japanese inns—*ryokans*—in Tokyo. The luxurious ones are out in the country. But when you get out of Tokyo, don't stay in anything but a *ryokan.*

The language barrier will be something. But you'll like it.

* * *

On local customs:

There's no tipping in Japan. (Except a matter of *Chadai* or tea money, which I'll explain later.)

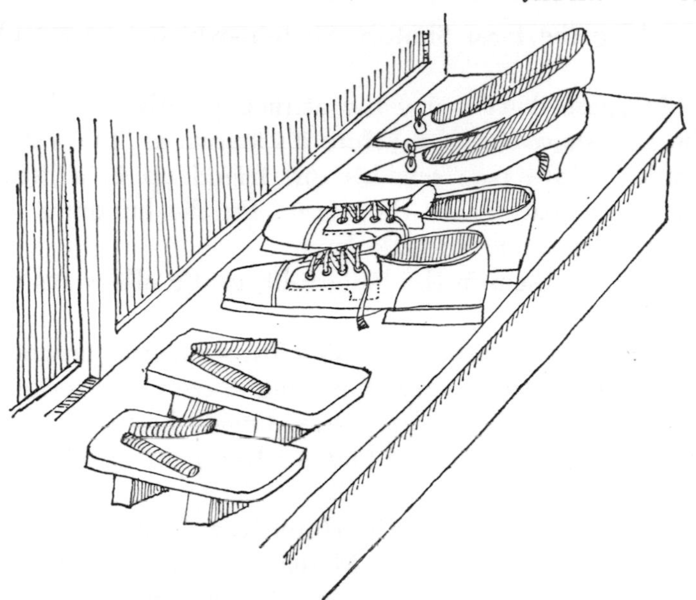

No tipping in your hotels. No tipping taxi drivers. No tipping waitresses.

Japanese bow at meeting and parting. You can do it, too. Put your palms on your knees and incline the head. (A half-nod is OK to acknowledge the bowing of maids.)

On entering Japanese houses, hotels, and restaurants, take off your shoes before you step on the floor at the entrance. Put on the slippers you see there. Before you enter a room with *tatami* (mats) take off the slippers.

Rule: No shoes on floors. No slippers on *tatami*.

Tokyo is the greatest night-life city in the world. It's estimated that there are 50,000 bars and night clubs—2000 in the 20-some blocks of the Ginza area alone.

Most of these are mama-san bars—the mama-san runs the bar. Three stools and one table. One girl-san to keep everybody company.

Drinks are about $1.50. You can do a little better

drinking the local Suntory Scotch—which is not bad at all.

Japanese don't marry the attractive girls who have been in show business. (Here it's known as "the water trade.") So a man sets his girl friend up in a little mama-san bar. That's the reason for the hundreds of these very attractive little bars.

You find them in the lantern-lit, exotic alleyways of the Ginza.

It's certainly worth an evening just wandering around.

There are some very plush night clubs. Luxurious decor. Great Filipino orchestras. Lovely hostesses—you pay them about $2.80 an hour (¥1000) for dancing or sitting with you.

The Latin Quarter in the Hotel New Japan. The elegant Copa Cabana run by Mama Cherry, who had the exclusive Cherry Club. The Monte Carlo in the Ginza district—about midnight they bring in 40 strip-tease girls who proceed to work on tables, balconies, and stairways. You never saw such mass production.

Don't miss the new Mikado. Two shows nightly. You can bring your wife.

There are a number of afternoon clubs that serve snacks, drinks, and a strip-tease show. A relaxed cocktail hour.

An interesting afternoon night-club sort of thing is the Japanese hot bath. (You find these advertised too.)

You drink, dance, or read the papers.

The finale is a Japanese hot soaking bath. Given to you by the hostess, who gets into a bathing suit for the event. It's certainly different.

* * *

A wonderful restaurant town. I never met anybody who couldn't get with Japanese food.

The restaurants are beautifully appointed. Usually

you have your own room. The guest of honor should sit with his back to the *takonoma*—that little alcove with a hanging scroll and a simple flower arrangement below it.

The major dishes:

Sashimi—raw fish, but you might learn to like it.

Yakitori—chicken broiled in sauce over charcoal. On a spit.

Various beef dishes. *Sukiyaki* is a good one to try.

Tempura—shrimp and vegetables fried in deep sesame seed oil. You usually sit at a counter for this. The Japanese feel that fish should be served immediately. Not carried from cooking place to the table.

You should try sake, the rice wine.

Custom on this is for ladies to hold the little cup with both hands. Men can hold it with one. But you *must* hold it while the waitress pours.

She'll keep refilling it. To stop this, turn it down on the table.

Japanese beer is excellent.

Take one evening and go into various little counter restaurants on the Ginza. Each serves a different specialty. Point to what you want—they don't speak English.

* * *

There are a number of good revues in town. You could start by trying Nichigeki, a few blocks from the Nikkatsu. A different show on every floor.

At the bottom, look for a black-as-pitch place with jazz booming out of loudspeakers. The waitresses light your cigarette by snapping the match out of a garter.

There are dozens of coffee and tea houses. Nicely decorated. Music in the afternoon. Inexpensive. Try the new Café Demi-tasse or the Sicilia on the opposite corner. Tako Horii even serves Irish coffee here! It's in the Roppongi District, about five minutes from the Okura and New Japan hotels. The area comes to life after midnight.

* * *

Traffic is left-handed. Your taxi driver is wild enough to give you gray hair within 20 blocks.

Taxis vary in price—*60* or *70* or *80* on the cab door indicates the price in yen of the flag drop. The pricing is done by the size of the cab. Little ones are cheaper.

Now—how do you get where you want to go? That is a good question.

Tokyo streets have only recently been named. The Occupation put up a few signs like *Avenue A* and *Annex Avenue.* Nobody pays attention to them. And a taxi driver wouldn't know what you were talking about.

Locations are done by districts and subdistricts. Then by visual landing. Houses are numbered only in the order in which they were built.

Local residents direct cabs by ordering the district and subdistrict. Then by reining the cabbie vocally—*hidari* (left), *migi* (right), *masugu* (straight ahead), *koko* (here).

On page 42 is a list of restaurants I know. With *phone numbers.*

When you find a place you like, pick up the house matches. Japanese pass out lots of little boxes of matches. Or take the paper cover off the *o-hashi*—the chopsticks—if it shows a phone number.

When you want to go back, show this to the driver.

Give him a 10-yen piece and say *denwa* (telephone). Or make a hand motion like phoning.

He gets the idea. He phones. They give him directions.

You'll never make it any other way.

* * *

The shopping is fabulous. Pearls, silver, silks, screens, carved furniture, cameras, transistor radios and TV sets, toys, binoculars.

There are a number of very big department stores. You could start along the Ginza. A very good place with the best merchandise is Wako.

You can have china made to order with your own design or name in Japanese (to ship it costs as much as the china itself, though).

As a foreigner, you don't have to pay the high internal-purchase tax.

But—you *must* have a currency-control slip, which you get from Customs on landing. They don't just hand this to you any more. You have to ask for it.

When you change money, have it entered on this slip.

When you purchase—in stores allowed to discount this tax—have them enter the purchase on this slip.

Some of the things I buy:

Pearls. I usually go to Mikimoto on the Ginza or the shops in the arcade of the Imperial or Nikkatsu hotels. I've heard you can do better with private salesmen. But I don't know pearls well enough to buy in the open market.

Silver cigarette cases, cases for Zippo lighters. Very inexpensive and good-looking.

Cufflinks made from the handle decorations on 250-year-old samurai swords. They are called *manuki.* You can get the originals at about $12. Or a just-as-good copy at $3. Japan Sword has them. It's listed in the guide *Tokyo This Week* on the hotel newsstand.

China—I bought a 12-place setting for about $50, made to my order.

Kimonos are very expensive, being to Japanese girls what Dior original evening gowns are to you.

Zoris—the handsome dress slipper-shoe. Inexpensive for women. Nice around the house.

Boy meets girl: Absolutely. Waitresses sit with you while you drink. So does your hotel maid. It is considered frightfully rude to let a man sit alone.

Japanese girls are raised to flatter and wait on men. This is so well known in the Orient that there is a saying:

"Catchee Japanese wife, Chinese cook, American paycheck. *Ichiban.* Number one."

There are hostesses in all the night clubs. And you are not very welcome if you don't have one come to your table. (Don't worry about cost. She gets $2.80 U.S. an hour—on your bill. This is not the champagne hustle you get in the world's clip joints.)

There are a few rules of decorum:

The greeter at the door says "good morning" instead of "good evening." A "good night" sort of welcome would be bad luck. Business is over.

Don't pinch the girl, no matter how friendly you feel. It's bad luck for her. No business. For good business and good luck, she carries a little pornographic charm. This is customary for everybody in "the water trade."

If you should touch her with a lighted cigarette accidentally, that's good luck.

Beside the front door, you'll see a little pile of salt. For "clean business."

If you come in, look around, and then go out, the owner will sprinkle salt at the door. Cleaning up the curse of such bad luck. (They do this after non-buying customers in stores.)

The chances that you will get to a geisha house are slim. Unless you have local friends.

Actually, there is no "geisha house." There are *ma-*

chiai—a sort of tea house with entertainment. The geishas are ordered from a central casting agency.

They sit with you. Drop a few current jokes. Play the *samisen* (which sounds like a cat on a love-sick night). Do a few dances which are flowers and poetry to watch. Figure about $30 per person in a top-grade *machiai*. Includes dinner.

A fine one is Cho-ya in the Akasaka district. But you have to be known or introduced and have reservations.

The geisha spends about six years learning the art. The best geisha comes from Kyoto. She is registered, pays a geisha tax. Usually she has several wealthy admirers contributing to the heavy expense of buying the best kimonos.

There are a few pseudo-geisha houses. During the American Occupation, geishas were in great demand. To fill it, the Japanese organized a sort of quick course—in a way equivalent to the Fort Benning 90-day Infantry officer-training course taken by the demanding clients.

Some of these still operate. The entertainers are delicately known as "pillow geishas."

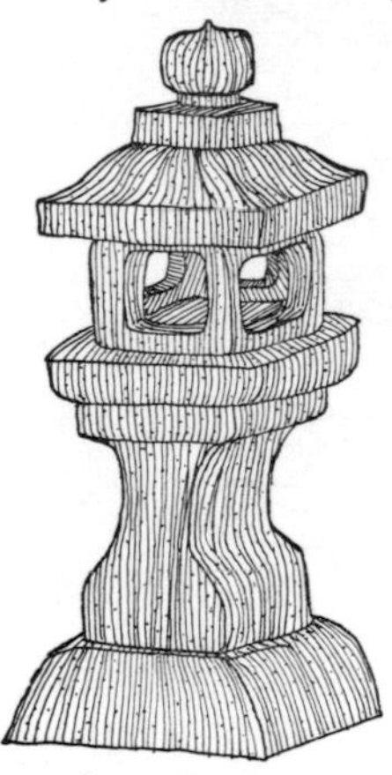

Tokyo Hotels

Akasaka Prince Hotel. A bit out of the heart of tourist Tokyo—in the Akasaka district. Good hotel, with lots going on. They have air conditioning. And the price is right. There's a dining room, grill, and a *tempura* counter. A night club, with dancing. A swimming pool. And guest golf privileges a 10-minute walk away. Be sure to specify a bath—some rooms don't have a private facility.

Imperial. The most famous—Frank Lloyd Wright designed the old wing. But stay in the new section if you like modern rooms. Especially in the summer. You'll need the air conditioning. The shopping arcade is fabulous. But prices are a little higher than you'll find around the corner. Good restaurants. And a sensational barber!

Tokyo Hilton. Conrad at his best. Long experience in the overseas hotel business makes this one of the better Hiltons.

Ginza Tokyu. The younger crowd seems to like this one. It's moderately priced, has nice rooms, and is well-located. Five semi-Japanese-style rooms if you want to try them. But reserve well in advance.

Dai Ichi. Small, inexpensivc. Two bars, a money exchange, and a souvenir shop. Spanish and German also spoken.

New Japan. A little out of the way of the central district. And the prices seemed high to me. It's pleasantly decorated and has good facilities and food.

Nikkatsu. On a busy downtown street. The shops around the hotel are not the most glamorous, but the price is right.

Okura. This is the newest. With the newest prices. Chinese and Japanese food.

Palace. Expensive and modern. Big rooms, good views of the Imperial Palace Plaza and downtown Tokyo. Near the Ginza.

If you want to live Japanese style, write the Japanese Ryokan Association at 1 Marunouchi, Chiyoda-Ku, Tokyo, or Japan Tourist Association at 651 Market

Street, San Francisco. They'll be happy to send you a good descriptive listing of the Japanese-style inns.

Tokyo Restaurants

Tokyo has every nationality represented in its hundreds of restaurants. But try the Japanese food before you sneak into the dining room of the Imperial for a steak just like you get at home.
Here's my private list. The places I visit:

For Tempura
Tsubaki Tempura Restaurant. One of the best and very colorful. Nihonbashi district, Naniwacho. Phone 671-7326.

For Tempura
Tsubohan Chazuke. Old-style farmhouse restaurant. Big hangout for Japanese movie stars, writers, etc. Get a reservation. And an introduction, if possible. Ginza Mishi district. Phone 571-0236 and 571-4737.

For O-sushi
Nakata's on the Ginza is king of the rice cakes.

For Sukiyaki

Doh-Hana Restaurant. (Pronounce it *Ski-yaki.*) Also *tempura* here. Very good and colorful. Gardens. Near Ueno Natsuzakaya department store. Phone 821-4037.

For Yakitori

Torishin Restaurant. Yakitori is chicken on a spit. Cooked over the hibachi with special sauce. Very, very good. Shibuya Dogenzaka Ue district. Phone 461-7565 and 461-7879.

For Pheasant

Akahene Restaurant. Greatest. Colorful. Gardens. Fried bees, bamboo shoots, wild duck, pheasant in plum wine. Akasaka Fukuyoshi-cho district. Get a reservation. Open only until 9 P.M. Phone 481-4023 and 481-4014.

For Yakitori

Miyakawa Sekiake Restaurant. More chicken on more spits. Near the Astor night club in Ginza Mishi district. Phone 571-1460.

For Pork Cutlet

Mutsumi Restaurant. Ask for tonkatsu. Downstairs in the Ginzakan. Ginza district. Phone 561-6340.

Genghis Khan Type

Ken Cole, a friend, suggests **Fu Jino.** Reservations required. Phone 591-6717.

Sicilia. Good Italian food. A favorite hangout for airline crews. Write your name on the ceiling with candle smoke. Phone 401-8054.

For American-style seafood, try Tokyo Kaikan Prunier. For steaks and chops try George's, the Suehiro Steak House, The Grill Rosini on Tokyo Kaikan.

The following places are so well known your hotel doorman will be able to direct the taxi driver:

Furusato. Country food in a Japanese-style farmhouse. 461-6515.

Ten-Ichi. Probably the best-known of the *tempura* bars. 571-1272 and 571-1949.

Sun-Ya. Northern Chinese cooking. I think it's one of the best. 431-4369.

Chinzanso Garden. You sit around a small outdoor grill. A Japanese waitress serves the pork, chicken, steak, onions, sweet potatoes, etc., all cut in the same designs and brushed with a delicious barbecue sauce. With hot sake.

Night Clubs and Entertainment

Coffee and tea houses usually have music. And are beautifully decorated. There are hundreds of small bars all along the Ginza, the Shinbashi district, and Asakusa Park. Beer and sake mostly. And lots of B-girls. You can drop a bundle.

Noh and Kabuki. The Kabuki Theater is on Z Street, and Noh (Kanze Noh Theater) in the Shinjuku district. For the classical plays of Japan.

All-girl revues—just like Las Vegas. The Asakusa Kokusai Theater for both Japanese and Western entertainment. Also the Takarazuka. Shinbashi Embujo for Japanese dances. And the Nichigeki Music Hall for pure Western style. These shows go on all day. Morning and afternoon. Last show is usually around 6 P.M.

For night clubs, I like:

The Queen Bee. For checking the action. There's a revolving bar. Hostesses stand around the bar in a circle. The young men peek into the back bar mirror, and when they come to a hostess they like, they simply turn around. Like getting the brass ring on a merry-go-round. Good show. Fair food.

Copa Cabana. In the Akasaka district. This has a great show. And the only night club I've ever been in where you can get a really good steak. Kobe beer-fed, hand-massaged beef, of course. This is quite a taxi jump from the Ginza. But it's worth it. You'll spend about $30 for dinner and drinks for two.

The Mikado. This is the place you can take your wife. (The other clubs have hostesses. They resent amateur competition.) Shows go on twice nightly—last one at about nine o'clock.

The main menu is fixed, cost for everything about $9.50 U.S.

The place holds 1500 and you see a lot of Japanese here. No dancing. Just the show, which features a line of French girls—this being pretty exotic in Japan—as well as the Japanese chorus girls.

Between the Imperial and Okura hotels in a side alley.

Club Hanabasha. On 10th between D and F. *Three* orchestras! All good. French and Chinese food. Two shows a night.

Casino Tokyo. On 10th near 5th. A friendly and informal Japanese-style cabaret. You won't have to look for others. Kick a Tokyo phone book and night clubs fall out for 20 minutes.

HOW TO GET THERE

Airlines: Air France, Air India, BOAC, Canadian Pacific, Cathay Pacific, CAT, Japan Air Lines, KLM Royal Dutch, Lufthansa, Northwest Orient, Pan American, Qantas, Thai Airway.

Steamship Lines: American Mail Line, American President Lines, P & O–Orient Lines, Pacific Far East Lines, Royal Interocean Lines.

ELECTRICAL CURRENT. 100 volts AC, in local hotels and homes. There is no need for special transformer plugs.

TO READ ALONG THE WAY. For background color, Fosco Mariani's *Meeting with Japan,* Oliver Statler's *Japanese Inn.*

FOR MORE INFORMATION. Pacific Area Travel Association, 442 Post Street, San Francisco; Japan National Tourist Association, 45 Rockefeller Plaza, New York City, and 651 Market Street, San Francisco. And your carrier.

Outside Tokyo

ATAMI

About an hour from Tokyo by fast, comfortable electric train. Don't drive in Japan. The roads are frightful. But the scenery is worth the train ride.

This is a seaside resort on the Izu Peninsula—a sort of Japanese Carmel or Cape Cod.

It has excellent Japanese inns. The streets are gay with Japanese holiday crowds in *yukatas* and the clackety-clack wooden *geta.* There are little pitchman games on the street. Little sake stands. (With a curtain halfway down so people can't see who's lushing it up this early in the morning).

An entertaining night life of dance pavilions, *machiais,* bars.

Japan is pretty relaxed about the homosexual. You'll find "gay boy" bars here as well as in the Shinbashi district in Tokyo. Lipstick and kimono.

The shops sell mostly tiny trinket souvenirs.

But it's a lively town. The Kiunkaku is a beautiful hotel with private gardens and excellent service. Plus the everybody-in-at-once community bath. It's not cold once you're in. In fact, it's so hot it will boil you. Go in easy.

And never with soap! You wash *outside* the tub. Rinse. Then go in and soak. Very chatty and probably the only time you'll see your fellow guests. Japanese inns have no lobby. Everybody lives privately. Except in the bath.

HAKONE

The Hakone Mountains are the cool summer resort away from Tokyo's muggy heat. Many good Japanese inns. Many lakes. Many Japanese walking tourists. (The cloth headband indicates determination.)

Choose an expensive *ryokan* ($15 a day with meals) from the Japanese Ryokan Association list. You'll live like a shogun.

NIKKO

A most unattractive town of little brown frame buildings. But it is Japanese custom to make the outside unattractive so you will appreciate more the beauty of the inside.

Simplicity is the key to beauty by Japanese thinking. The flower arrangement. The tea ceremony. The few lines on the scroll in your room. All are done with a minimum of line.

You come to Nikko to see the impressive temples erected in the glory of the shogunate, the military caste who ruled Japan in her greatest flowering of culture.

Interesting. But I wouldn't go twice.

Konishi Bekkan is a very pleasing small inn. With a view and a good lunch for ¥500 ($1.40).

KYOTO

The old Japanese capital. Traditional home of the geisha. Excellent restaurants.

American bombers didn't hit Kyoto. Consequently it is Old Japan.

Wonderful restaurants overlooking the river. The roast lamb Genghis Khan is a specialty.

The geisha schools hold open classes in the tea ceremony. And there is a fine geisha theater. The apprentice geisha is known as a *maiko*. You see them here, learning the trade. It's a sight you shouldn't miss.

I would visit Kyoto again and again.

Try the little alleys running off the canals (where Marlon Brando made *Sayonara*). Full of surprising exotic bars, restaurants.

Kyoto Restaurants

Suehiro. For Kobe beef. Try the queen steak here.

Sa-Ami. For sukiyaki and other Japanese specialties. Located in pretty Maryuama Park.

Karafune. Another plush Japanese style. Off with the shoes!

Mishimatei. More of the same. Good, Japanese.

Hiromasha. Small tempura bar in the Gion section. Sit on wooden stools, watch the owner dip the shrimp. You can have 12 different fish courses. Great mushrooms. Try the hot sake here.

Hotels

Atami: Kiunkaku Hotel. I stayed here. And I like it. Out on the Izu Peninsula about an hour's ride from Tokyo by electric train. You'll have your own garden. A happy Japanese resort.

Beppu: Kamenoi Hotel. Both Japanese- and Western-style rooms. Natural hot-spring baths. Moderate prices.

Hakone: Fujiya Hotel. On a hillside. Sixteen acres of landscaped gardens. Specify Japanese- or Western-style baths. I like the Japanese. Lots to do. Swimming pools indoors and out. Tennis, golf. Good arcade of shops.

Kyoto: Miyako Hotel. Modern, very elegant. Plenty of garden here, too. Dining room, grill, sukiyaki room. Three bars. Geisha, *maiko* dances, Noh plays, flower-arrangement demonstrations, and tea ceremonies, on request. Golf, tennis, swimming.

Kyoto: Tanaraya Inn. Japanese inn, 200 years old. Excellent.

Tours

The Japanese themselves are great on organized tours. This demand plus the language barrier for foreigners makes tours desirable. The lovely idea of just browsing around works in Europe. But you'd better get some guided insulation in Japan.

The Japanese are friendly enough. But they aren't socially elastic.

You can use the wrong bathroom but not the wrong word.

A social mistake in Japan throws the whole economy into a big swivet. You're likely to find everybody taking off in all directions to think about it. Restore the balance. Meantime, there you are, standing with the ticket in hand and nowhere to go.

Japan Air Lines helped me with a lot of this tour information. They're the best source I know for getting around Japan without getting your feet wet.

* * *

Now the tours. They're good, well organized. Your guides speak English and are as polite as if they owed you money.

They are usually classified de luxe, standard, or economy.

The difference is usually in the quality of hotel—but some economy tours go third-class train, which are clean and swift. But they left the plush off the seats.

De luxe tours usually throw in a geisha party.

For guided tours for Westerners, the geishas do the dance routine—the one about Okichi, supposed to have been the mistress of Townsend Harris, America's first envoy, is a favorite.

It's all very chaste since you have ladies on the tour. And the Japanese guide tells you how the geisha is *not* what you so deliciously thought. No, she is an entertainer with a moral code of a Girl Guide.

This is so much wind-in-the-willows. The geisha needs several steady friends just to keep her in those $500-to-$1000 kimonos. It is all very moral from the Japanese viewpoint. But not from the Western idea—hence the guide will dress it up to suit your fancy.

The geisha *is* primarily an entertainer in dancing, the *samisen* and so on. She pays a geisha tax and is booked through a central casting agency.

Even in the sterilized version, catch a geisha party. It's a pistol. Catch plenty of Japanese dinners in the sit-down style. The food is delicious. The serving is magnificent. Japanese feel that sight is as important as flavor or fragrance. Each dish is presented as carefully as a flower arrangement.

Catch a flower arrangement. Have it explained to you.

All flower arrangements are done with a basic philosophy—Heaven and Earth joined by Man.

Try to get a tour that gives you one night in a *ryokan* —a Japanese inn.

Be sure to get a Japanese deep-dish bath—even if you don't go for the community model.

Get a massage. They go for $1 at the highest. You can get them in your room.

Afternoon Tokyo Tour ($2.80 U.S.)

By sightseeing bus is good enough. Takes you to the Imperial Palace, where Emperor Hirohito is still in residence. To Korakuen Garden—it was landscaped for the shoguns, the military caste who ruled Japan during its great flowering of the arts.

The garden has the classic full-moon bridge and a small temple on the island in the lake. To the judo studio, where you can see the experts flip each other around like campfire pancakes.

Through the enormous Asakusa entertainment district. (They probably won't take you into these places, but here are the strip shows of the world. Hundreds of them.)

To the ancient temple of Kannon. The image of the Goddess of Mercy is supposed to have appeared in a fisherman's net 1400 years ago.

Return to the Ginza for tea in the big Mitsukoshi department store.

(*Tip:* Take the elevator to the top floor and walk down. Good shopping.)

Tokyo All-Day Tour ($5.60 U.S.)

Same as afternoon tours (there are several, visiting different points of interest). The all-day tour includes a Japanese garden lunch and a modern Japanese revue at the Kokusai Theater. Night-club tours go on from here at prices from $11 to $23.

Tokyo Special Tours ($3.60–$7)
A "Seven Wonders" trip (Sunday only, $7) gives you a tea-house luncheon with classic dancers. You see the Tokyo Tower—something like the Eiffel Tower but higher. The Folkcraft Museum, three outstanding Buddhist temples, and the famous Shinto shrine at Ueno.

There is an afternoon art tour ($4.20) that visits a *bonseki* (tray landscape) and woodblock studios. Goes on to a *Bonsai*-tree garden exhibit, a ceramics studio, and a formal tea ceremony at a Japanese inn. (This is something to see!)

There are garden tours (Mondays, $4.20) and a cultural tour (Wednesdays, $3.60) that shows handicrafts, music, and classic dancing—all with English explanation.

Nikko Tour ($15 for one day, $30 for two)
The Japanese say, "Never use the word *magnificent* until you have seen Nikko."

The temple complex is magnificent. The town is pretty dingy, so don't expect the Las Vegas Strip. Hotels are good. I thought a little colorless contrasted to the flaming temples across the river, but OK.

The tour includes a cable-car ride up to the crater lake of Chuzenji. A ferryboat trip on the lake, the curving ride to the waterfall, and an elevator ride down.

The shrines built by the Toshugu shoguns are brilliantly decorated and the feature attraction of Nikko.

No use describing them. Go look. Wonderful red bridge across the river. Take plenty of color film. Flashbulbs for the interiors.

In the Japanese winter, Nikko gets some skiers.

Kamakura Tour ($15 for one day)

Thirty miles south of Tokyo, can be done in one day. This is where you see the 42-foot bronze Daibutsu Buddha, which has done more for Eastman film than Carter's pills did for your liver.

Even the Japanese snap their cameras at this. And rare is the Japanese travel folder or magazine that doesn't picture it.

There is a stairway inside. You can walk up as high as the shoulders.

You can buy various excursions to Kamakura—via Yokohama, with a morning of sightseeing, or a drive along the colorful Enoshima seacoast. I recommend the seacoast drive. Yokohama is just another seaport. Both $15 out of Tokyo.

Fuji–Hakone Tour ($15 for one day by train from Tokyo)

This is a great national park area, cool in the hot summer. Therefore it has some of the best Japanese inns in the whole country.

Your tour, however, will probably put you up in a Western hotel. It is the firm belief of the Japanese that you will be horrified at sleeping in a bed on the floor. You may not win, but you could ask when you book.

Lots of boiling geysers, sulphur springs, and other things of the Yellowstone Park variety.

The main advantage, I think, is the mountain scenery and mountain air. Especially in summer, when Tokyo is hot as a TV sheriff's pistol.

Lovely Fuji lakes ($25 for a two-day visit). You see five of the scenic lakes and go to the fifth station of Mount Fuji (the climb is marked with numbered stations).

There are several tours in the Fuji–Hakone region. If you have the two days, take one. About $30 tops from Tokyo and return.

Old Tokaido Road Tour ($65 U.S. for three days)

To keep the Japanese from moving around too much or gathering in dissident groups, the military shoguns kept only one road—the Tokaido. (They locked the imperial family in a castle in Kyoto and moved the government to Tokyo.)

You had to have a license to travel on the Tokaido, and they kept it in bad condition at that. Japanese roads still are frightful. Don't rent a car. Take a train. They're great.

This is a motor-coach tour from Tokyo to Kamakura to Hakone to Nagoya over the Tokaido road. You stop at Minaguchiya—have you read Oliver Statler's *Japanese Inn?* Well, read it. It's the story of the Minaguchiya and the Tokaido road.

At Shizuoka you get steaks. (They massage the cattle and feed them beer. Talk about contented cows!)

At Nagoya, they take you to the city's Castle of the Golden Dolphins. Also shopping at the local porcelain and cloisonné factories.

Nagaragawa River Tour ($3.40 from Nagoya)

This is worth the time and money. This is where the cormorant fishermen turn loose these birds to dive for fish. The cormorant has a ring around his neck—a withholding tax: He can't swallow the fish. The fisherman gets that.

As a reward, the cormorant gets the ring taken off and swallows every seventh fish, a ratio a great deal like our higher tax brackets.

This tour is only June through August. The river is full of Japanese and the Japanese are full of sake. The boats are lantern-lit and a merry time is had by all. Except the poor one-in-seven cormorant.

Kyoto Tour ($98 for five days)
I recommend this one. Motor coach up the Tokaido road with stops as above. There is a detour to see Ise-Shima, the Mecca of Shintoism, with unpainted wooden temples where the Emperor worships.

You also stop at Mikimoto Pearl Island where Japanese women dive for the oysters in which cultured pearls have been planted. (They used to wear just goggles and shorts. But I hear that since it has become such a popular tour stop, they have added bras.)

You go on through Kamakura, Hakone, Nagoya, and wind up with two days of sightseeing in Kyoto, Nara, and Osaka.

Kyoto is most colorful. Nara has a temple and sacred deer. Osaka is industrial and not much. Great night-life town, though.

Around Kyoto ($2.80 for the afternoon)
Kyoto is seven hours south of Tokyo by a bus-and-train combination. Or you can fly it with Japan Air Lines in an hour and 20 minutes for $15.90.

Plenty of independent local tours available through your hotel desk.

The afternoon tour takes you to the Higashi Honganji Temple. The pagoda towers of Nijo Castle. The old Imperial Palace. The delicate 14th-century golden pavilion of Kinkakuji Temple.

Morning tours ($2.80) visit Sanjudangendo Temple with the thousand-handed image of the goddess Kannon and a thousand-and-one statues of holy women. Goes on to Kiyomizu Temple, cantilevered out from a cliff overlooking the valley. Then to Heian Shinto Shrine, a colorful garden-temple complex.

Tremendous displays of statuary and paintings.

There is an excellent night tour ($8.40) during which you get a look at the *maiko,* the apprentice geishas.

The night tour takes you to Shoren-In Temple, where you hear harp music three centuries old. (Practically pop music in ancient Japan.) You follow with a night club with a floor show.

The topper is the dinner at a Japanese restaurant with the *maiko.*

An afternoon garden tour ($3.40) and an all-day cultural tour—of paintings, dancing, etc. ($8.40)—can be bought during the summer tourist season.

* * *

Less than an hour from Kyoto you can shoot the rapids of the Hozu River. It's as safe as the Tunnel of Love in an amusement park but a lot more thrilling. Round trip from Kyoto $3.40.

Odd Tours

One day from Kyoto to Nara with the Inari Shrine and the sacred deer park; lunch at Nara Hotel. $6.10.

The night tour of Osaka costs $10 and takes you to three cabarets. Includes the Metro, which has three simultaneous floor shows—like a three-ring circus.

From Kobe, a seaport an hour by train from Kyoto, you take a steamer on the Inland Sea trip. Two-day tour costs $33.40. Three-day tours are $75, with an overnight at the ancient Dogo spa. The local castle has the best collection of samurai choppers in Japan. Old armor museum.

The trips on the Inland Sea can be extended to Hiroshima.

Also available on this run is the southernmost island, Kyushu, and the Beppu hot springs. Eight kinds of mineral baths. Hot sand baths on the beach. It's on the ocean; you can swim.

A five-day tour of the northern island of Hokkaido is now on the market. You visit a village of Ainus, the aborigines of Japan. Mountain resorts are a big thing and few tourists get on this unbeaten path.

* * *

All Japan tours can usually be booked through your hotel desk. Any travel agency has them. Japan Air Lines has some excellent booklets on language and customs.

If you want to do something the agencies don't have, call 502-1461 (Tokyo).

This is the Japan National Tourist Association. They talk English at the Association. That will help.

No bookings. But they tell you how to do it.

AND ANOTHER THING

You wonder why the Japanese agent keeps pushing you on Western-style hotels?

First, he thinks you won't like the sleep-on-the-floor, sit-on-the-floor life. (But there's usually an alcove overlooking the garden with table and chairs if you want to change.)

Second, many Japanese inns advertise in Western magazines to give them "face." But if they take you, the Western visitor, and you don't know enough to take your shoes off, they are faced with a terrible problem.

If they tell you to take your shoes off, they are impolite.

If they let you leave them on, that's terrible, too.

So they advertise to get face. Refuse to take you for fear of losing face. About the only way is to get a knowledgeable agent who will fill you in and guarantee you.

* * *

Once in, you don't have to go for the community bath. You can get a private bath.

Service is included as 10 per cent of the bill in all hotels—and restaurants.

But in a *ryokan*—not in the Western hotels—you can give *cha-dai*. Tea money. (About 5 per cent additional.)

Get your personal room maid to get you some gift envelopes. They are specially decorated. She will mark them up. The bath boy gets a little. I think the chef gets a little. Maybe the phone girl.

She will tell you how much for each.

For her? I never could get them to do more than giggle. So I give her double whatever was most in the other envelopes.

You envelope the money of course. It is considered very bad manners to hand over raw money.

The hotel will probably give you a going-away present. Usually a handkerchief—by the way, you don't open gifts in front of the giver.

Only give handkerchiefs for good-by presents. Handkerchiefs are to cry in, see?

Oh, yes. On that tipping. Ship and airport porters live on tips. One hundred yen per bag, not in envelopes but out of pocket, is right.

And the night club hostess might hustle a tip on top of her hourly fee.

Pay it.

To call the waitress or waiter, say *choto* (both *o*'s as in *so*).

They are also called "girl-san" and "boy-san."

Arigato—accent on the last *a*—is "thank you."

For "please," say *dozo*.

After that? In the words of the immortal Knute Rockne: "When in doubt, punt!"

HONG KONG

"Chinese dress must not open upstairs. Only open downstairs."

. . . The first who set the example of a stone and brick house was Mr. Matheson; Government soon after commenced the magistracy and prison, and others followed in their train, and now few Europeans think of a palm-leaf house, except with certain forebodings of fever and ague. Hawkers of every description abound, as well as the various sorts of fortune tellers, jugglers, quacks, and actors, that are seen in all well populated Chinese towns.

. . . The population has often been estimated at 15,000 souls: and it is probable that this number is by no means an over-estimate. There are not more than a dozen horses on the island, and one carriage; a few small flocks of sheep and some goats.

Many of the complaints about excessive heat, and excessive cold and dreadful unhealthiness, are being forgotten, except among those who have little else to occupy their attention—amidst the general bustle and activity of Hong Kong. Just now whilst trade at Canton continues open and unmolested, that carried on at Hong Kong is of little consequence, and chiefly confined to opium, and here and there a few manufactured goods may be disposed of, or a little tea and cassia purchased.

—from articles in the Canton Press, *1842*

MONEY. Shifts; around $5.71 HK to $1 U.S.

BEST TIME TO GO. September–February.

LANGUAGE. English is official since this is a Crown Colony under perpetual treaty (except for the New Territories, which revert to China in a few decades).

Since it *is* China, though, the language of the streets is Cantonese, the rolling, singsong Chinese of the sunny south.

There's little chance you will use it. I've never picked up a single Chinese word—just no reason to.

The Cantonese are the wayfarers of China. Their restaurants and laundries steam from the Golden Gate to Piccadilly.

They run all the business in the South Pacific, thanks to the *hui* or family corporate setup. Lee goes to the Philippines and sets up a sari-sari store. When he makes enough, he imports a cousin to run the store while he dabbles in the rice market.

Soon there is a spreading family of Lees, interlocking in buying and selling and financing.

This traveling has produced a ship's pidgin English on the shoreside Cantonese of Hong Kong.

"Small chow" means *hors d'oeuvre.*

"Fish eggs topside" means caviar on toast.

"Look out below" for "be careful."

The English of Hong Kong speak with the Haymarket accent and a liberal use of the adjective *bloody,* and recognize each other by the gin-and-tonic habit and the white shorts at sundown. Society is pretty stuffy, eckchally.

The Crown Colony is built on an island with a heavy spillover into Kowloon on the mainland side. Some 3,000,000 people, with an uncounted daily increase

floating down the Pearl River or jumping the wire at the border.

In spite of overcrowding and poverty, the Chinese are resilient. Full of jokes—usually on the rough side. Energetic, hard-working. You see hunger in Hong Kong but not despair, want but not hopelessness.

It's exciting, Oriental, full of sharp smells and exotic sights.

There is no more beautiful sight than the homeward traffic of bat-winged fishing junks at evening. The sun powdering the harbor with gold. The Nine Dragon hills black against the sky. And the sprinkle of lights rising from the Hong Kong waterfront to the elegant homes on The Peak.

* * *

Take health precautions here. Cholera drifts in with the refugees—the British inoculate, but many Chinese fear the foreign devil's needle and hide.

I go to Hong Kong with a full yellow card—cholera

shots, typhoid shots, smallpox vaccination. And if you enter from certain areas, you'll need yellow-fever inoculations.

Drink bottled water and don't eat uncooked fruit or vegetables except in the very best restaurants and hotels.

Hong Kong is always short on water. On the back of your bathroom door, there's a schedule when water is turned on. That's why your room boy keeps the bathtub full. (There's a saucepan alongside to refill the flush tank of the toilet.)

Water is usually turned off from 10 A.M. to 4 P.M. Also during the night. Plan your baths accordingly.

If you should pick up the local dysentery, a non-prescription pill called Entero-vioform usually takes care of it. If it doesn't, see a doctor.

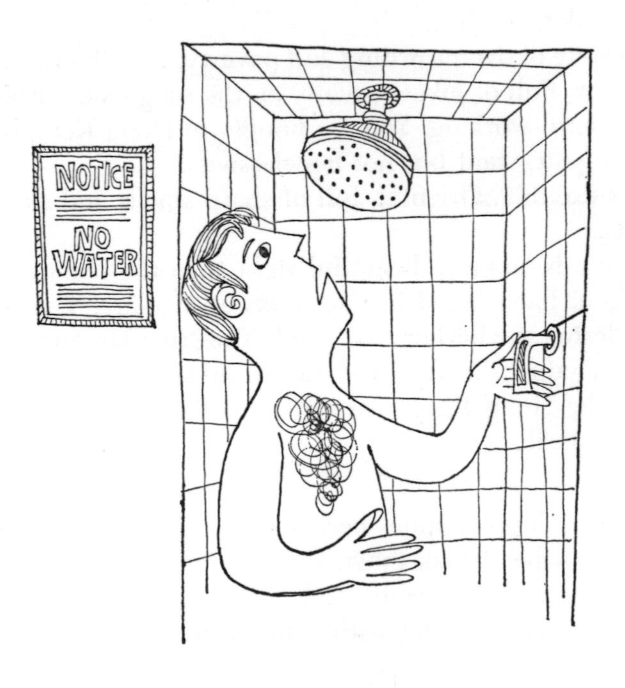

Plenty of good British and Chinese doctors for emergencies. And drugstores as well equipped as those of London. They may have a few dried sea horses and herbs for the Chinese trade. But they keep penicillin on the shelf, too.

* * *

Hong Kong is the great eating and shopping town of the Orient. The Cantonese are such good cooks that there is a proverb: "Canton to eat, Suchow to marry, Luchow to die." (Suchow has the prettiest girls and Luchow is famed for its coffins.)

* * *

Customs are British, polite but stiff. Heaven help you if you arrive without proper papers. I forgot to get a visa once. They let me in after a while. But they also made me appear at police headquarters every day I was in the Colony. British citizens (including Canadians) need no visa. U.S. citizens distinctly do.

You'll probably stay on the Kowloon (mainland) side. The Star Ferry runs across every 10 minutes for 20 Hong Kong cents. Nice clean craft—and on its scrubbed benches the best place to see the slit-skirt *cheongsam* in all its slit splendor.

Tipping is 10 per cent of the restaurant or taxi bill.

Give your room boy about $3 HK the first day. Same at the end of the week.

Don't put your handbag down when you are shopping. And don't keep your wallet in your hip pocket.

Although Hong Kong likes to bill itself "the shopper's Paradise," you can pay a number of prices to get into this heaven.

British stores like the excellent Lane, Crawford department store have one price.

Chinese and East Indian shops have a dozen.

Bargaining is the spice of the Orient. What we would call cheating the customer, is considered worthy and admirable here. (Our fierce business competition, which sometimes drives a small merchant out of work, the Chinese consider immoral. You must not "break a man's rice bowl.")

About the only way I've found to bargain around these shops is (1) know what the article is worth to you, or (2) offer half of whatever is asked. If the bid is accepted rapidly, you've been had.

The best buys go on forever: silks, ivory, carved teak chests. Handmade blouses, shirts, silk robes, clothing tailor-made from the best English materials.

Brass, wrought iron, a complete sailing junk made of teak if you like.

It's a free port. No duty. German cameras are less than they are in Germany. Swiss watches are less than in Switzerland. Japanese radios are cheaper than in Tokyo.

There's one catch for the American buyer: You can't buy things made in Communist China and bring them back to the States.

The British don't have such a rule. So shops are

loaded with Shanghai silk—silk made in Red China. Rugs from Szechuan. Carved chests for a song—but you can't hit the right tune to get them past U.S. Customs at Honolulu.

Anything you get here has to have a certificate of origin—attesting it was made in Hong Kong—from the U.S. Consulate.

All the shops know this and know how to get the certificates.

Some shopkeepers will insist that a simple letter from them will get it passed. It won't.

* * *

There are a thousand Chinese tailors in Hong Kong. Making clothing is a big thing in the Colony.

Sweatshop labor is cheap and English materials come in duty-free. So also do cheap Japanese imitations—some of it nicely labeled *Made in England.*

The "we make in 24 hours" is never, never going to look good on you. Unless it's a pair of pajamas.

The good tailors need at least five days of fittings. Do it this way and for $50 you'll have a suit that would cost you $200 at home.

I've been using Jimmy Chen for men's clothing. Frank Fong for women's things. Benny's for making shoes.

Tailor Cheong has a good reputation. Lane, Crawford has a good tailor. There are several good English tailoring firms.

The shopping is an adventure—you never know just how you'll come out.

There seems to be a little racket among the guide services. As it is all over the world, guides get a percentage of what you buy. In Hong Kong, there has been some scandal about the way things are marked up to take care of the guides.

Local correspondents advised me to let the guides do the guiding. You do your own shopping.

Chinese restaurants go for bright lights, carved red dragons, and lots and lots of courses.

The ones that will interest you most are at Aberdeen, a short ride from town. The famous floating restaurants.

A water-taxi girl will scull you out to them. They are like big, bright ferryboats of San Francisco vintage years.

The dinner is fish, of course. You choose your own from the fish swimming in fish tanks sunk off the side of the boat. (I sometimes think these fish are props. Used to be they lifted the catch in front of you and threw it to a chef on a cooking barge alongside. Now they lift out your choice. But I think they throw it back when you go upstairs.)

The food is delicious. A good chef cooks only one special dish and gets about $1000 HK per month.

You need a guide (or a Chinese friend) to do a night tour of the Typhoon Shelter. You do this with the sculled sampans.

The Shelter is where the junks tie up at night on the water streets.

They are serviced by floating delicatessens. There are streets of what are delicately called "flower girls." There are floating mah jongg games. Floating schools and floating temples.

It's a life of the Water People on the water. A different people who live and die on the tides of the sea where it meets the Pearl River.

For in-town eating, the Parisian Grill is modern and very good. You can get a martini chilled to the American taste.

The cheap caviar that used to come in from Harbin is no longer available. But they do bring in the tasty, live Sydney rock oysters from Australia.

Maxim's has good food and music.

Marco Polo has a small dance floor, good food. Luxurious and somewhat expensive.

Jimmy's Kitchen is up a dark alley. Very popular. Better reserve on week ends.

If you can get your guide to take you mornings to a

tea house, you'll see the Chinese businessman's operation. All the news filters through the tea houses. Steamed, meat-filled buns and tea is the fare. Delicious.

* * *

Boy meets girl: At the various ballrooms. Filipino orchestras are excellent. Filipinos are the troubadors of the Orient. The girls are pretty. Costs about $11 HK an hour to sit or dance with them. Tennochy is probably the best.

The routine is interesting. The chief hostess brings you a listing of the girls. You mark your choice by putting an *X* beside her name.

Since you don't know any of them, there's a sort of blind-date spice about this. You can ask her out to dinner—they take a dinner break. It gives her face, too. Face being very, very important in the Orient.

The little dance clubs in the Wanchai dock area are sailor joints and can get pretty rough. Only for the adventurous.

But I would take a look at the **Luk Kwok Hotel** in this district.

This was the locale of *The World of Suzie Wong.*

The book and the movie drew so much carriage trade that the hotel was bought by a Chinese millionaire. He put in air conditioning and a Chinese cowboy orchestra playing "Home on the Range" songs.

All this chi-chi has driven out the original hairy-chested British seamen who were the clientele of Suzie Wong times. But it's still fun to visit.

Al Kay, who press-agents for Pan American Airways, tells me it's a good hotel to stay in. Good prices and good rooms. But it isn't the best district.

* * *

If you ask a Chinese friend to do something for you and he can't do it, you will be told he is sick. Or he had to go visit relatives in China.

He would lose face if he told you he couldn't do it.

He would lose face if he didn't do it.

So he avoids the whole problem. (I have been waiting for an answer to a letter for more than a year. My friend is still "sick." He couldn't do what I asked.)

Face is important to your room boy.

If you have importance at home, let him know it. This gives him face from the face you have.

Mimi Lau, a Chinese newspaperwoman, met friends of mine at the airport.

"I give you big face with your friends," she reported.

When a Chinese millionaire or your room boy offers to do something, let him do it. He loses face if you don't. Gets face if you accept.

Most women fall at some time into the engaging slit skirt called a *cheongsam*.

If you are slim, you can do it.

If you are not, don't.

The slim, long-legged Chinese girls look wonderful in them. But they don't export unless you have the figure. *Cheongsams* are made wonderfully and cheaply here.

Chinese men, by the way, are not particularly intrigued with this leggy display. Maybe a matter of too much cake.

But let a girl finger the high collar and they are all attention.

A Chinese girl explained it this way:

"Chinese dress must not open upstairs. Only open downstairs."

New Territories

This extra land under lease to the British is part of Hong Kong's rice bowl.

The drive takes a leisurely half-day. You can get within sightseeing distance of Red China. Close enough to see a few gray-uniformed, sullen border guards.

When the refugees are allowed to cross (who knows why Red China relaxes on this?) you'll see them on the roads. If they are coming across, better take a bagful of rice cakes. It will break your heart anyway.

Macao

A Portuguese colony on the edge of Red China and a smuggling port of great importance to both sides.

A good steamship, the *Tak Shing*, runs over in about three hours. (Notice the barbed wire rimming the bridge. To keep pirate-minded passengers from swarming up and taking over the ship.)

There are a couple of good hotels.

The town is wide open—gambling, brothels, opium dens.

You can walk right up to the border here. Portuguese and Chinese border guards stand only a few feet apart.

Hotels

Two new hotels opened on the Hong Kong side in 1963. The **Mandarin Hotel** and the **Hong Kong Hilton.** I haven't seen either one.

The hotel at Repulse Bay is good too. With swimming. But it's not the best location for the tourist. Too far out of town. You're in a taxi most of the time checking in and out of town for shopping and sightseeing. And you'll be taken there on a tour anyway.

Most visitors stay on the mainland (Kowloon) side. Here's my pick:

Ambassador. Air-conditioned from penthouse to Cellar bar. There is a five-piece band in the European-style dining room. Five bars. A Spanish trio in the Cellar. Free golf for guests on a course a half-hour's drive away.

Astor Hotel. A fair hotel with fair prices. Air conditioning, too.

August Moon. New, small hotel. Rooms are good size. And the view from the front rooms is a good one of the Bay and downtown. When I ate there the service was pretty slow.

Carlton Hotel. I practice my Spanish here. Staff also speak Portuguese and Malay. All air-conditioned. Night club. And free transportation downtown every half-hour. Plans for a seven-story annex which may be finished when you arrive. Looks good to me.

Hotel Miramar. OK rooms. French and Japanese spoken, as well as English. Night club with Chinese floor shows that are usually good. Food is as good as hotel food gets. And the location is fine for shopping on a walk-around basis. A 15-story wing set for 1963.

Imperial Hotel. Modern, new hotel next to Ambassador; small, well-furnished rooms. Front rooms have view of the bay. Completely air-conditioned. Night club.

Park Hotel. Front rooms command glorious views of the harbor. New, all air-conditioned. Arcade of shops. Two dining rooms.

Peninsula Hotel and Marco Polo Peninsula Court. The Peninsula probably has one of the most famous hotel lobbies in the world. (Don't worry, it's being redecorated.) The Court is around the corner. All air-conditioned. Best restaurants, too: the famous Gaddi's in the Peninsula and the Marco Polo in the Court. French,

German, Italian, Russian, Portuguese, and—of course—English spoken.

Grand Hotel. Inexpensive. In the heart of the shopping district. Rooms are small. But clean and adequate.

And then there's the new **President Hotel.** Definitely luxurious, with 850 rooms.

Restaurants

Gaddi's. One of the leading grocery stores in the Orient. Excellent wine list. In the Peninsula Hotel.

Marco Polo. Like a U.S. supper club. Luxury from the menu to the orchestra. And a shuffleboard-size dance floor.

Jimmy's Kitchen. On the Hong Kong side. Take the Star Ferry and walk from there. You go up a narrow, dark alley. Clamorous but not dangerous. Food is very good, so you should reserve a table. Especially on week ends.

Parisian Grill. French food. And Irish coffee! Dark as a yard up a stovepipe. This is another dark-alley walk if you really want that Hong Kong feeling. There's a piano.

Princess Garden. Most popular for visitors interested in Chinese food. Better check for reservations. Floor show and dancing after dinner.

Try one of the floating restaurants at Aberdeen. Prices are high. But it's worth the expenditure.

Shopping

Trying to run down shopping in Hong Kong is like counting sand. You never run out. Just remember to get the Comprehensive Certificate of Origin to prove your purchases were made in Hong Kong, not in China. You'll need it for linens, silk, ivory, jade, brocades, carpeting, and furniture. The certificate costs about 75 cents and covers up to $1500 worth of merchandise from the same store.

Most of the shops open about 10 A.M. and close at 9 P.M.

Tours probably have been arranged for you in advance. The best sightseeing is the Hong Kong Island tour, which pulls you up Victoria Peak on a cable car, around the island to Repulse Bay for lunch and a walk through the local Disneyland—Tiger Balm Gardens.

If you're with your wife, be careful of some of the stereo slides for sale. They're not all scenery. I was amazed!

Be sure to see the New Territories. And Typhoon Anchorage.

* * *

No point in bringing in either liquor or cigarettes. Both are cheap in this free-port economy.

Being British Colonial, Hong Kong is dressy. Absolutely coat and tie in the evening. Cocktail gowns for the women. Keep it summer weight (except during the few chill rainy winter months). Hong Kong can be hotter than a firecracker. A dampish, muggy heat.

One of those Japanese folding umbrellas fits your luggage. You can buy them here. And it's better than a raincoat, which will leave you dry from rain but soaking from perspiration.

HOW TO GET THERE

Airlines: Air France, Air India, BOAC, Canadian Pacific, Cathay Pacific, CAT, Japan Air Lines, Lufthansa, Malayan Airways, Pan American, Philippine Air Lines, Qantas, Thai Airways.

Steamship Lines: American Mail Line, American President Lines, Java Pacific & Hoegh Lines, P & O–Orient Lines, Pacific Far East Lines, Royal Interocean Lines.

ELECTRIC CURRENT. Voltage is 220 A.C. Transformer plugs needed.

TO READ ALONG THE WAY. *The World of Suzie Wong* by Richard Mason, *A Many-Splendored Thing* by Han Suyin, *Peony* by Pearl Buck, *Jade* by the Hong Kong Tourist Association, *Hong Kong* by Harold Ingraham.

There are more shopping guides to Hong Kong than any other place in the world.

FOR MORE INFORMATION. PATA (Pacific Area Travel Association), 442 Post Street, San Francisco. And your carrier.

Tours

Since Hong Kong and the leased New Territories butt right up against Red China, there isn't a great deal of touring room. The tour of rural New Territories can only be stretched to four and a half hours—60 road miles and a long-distance peek over the Bamboo Curtain.

However, downtown Hong Kong and Kowloon (where most of the luxury hotels are located) can give quite a sight in a daily walking tour.

Sad to say, Hong Kong is generally hot and humid. You wear out in a few blocks. But there are a number of places to stop for a beer. (Locally brewed Philippine San Miguel and imported Danish Carlsberg seem to be the leaders.)

The 10-minute ferry ride from Hong Kong to Kowloon is cooling.

The Colony has now grown to 3,000,000—and that's a British guess.

Crowded but colorful.

More Chinese than ever before; the British are immersed in the flood of immigration.

Red China shadows the Colony. Its goods are in the shops. Its bank is the tallest in the Colony. Its political influence is a constant pressure.

Not every refugee is a disillusioned hater of communism by a long shot.

A good many are here only because the economy looks like a better deal—for the time being.

If you think the Hong Kong Chinese look upon you as a bastion against a slave world or a last hope, you are much mistaken.

You are a tourist with tourist values. You may tip. You may buy. You may stay long and enrich your guide. You may go tomorrow and leave him with a day's wages. Your political status doesn't enter into it.

New Territories Tour ($5–$8; Minibus or sedan)
This covers 60 miles of rural farming country which the Crown Colony has under lease from China for a few more years.

It's the only look you get at rural China: rice paddies, the Chinese farmhouses with homemade rush raincoats hanging on the wall. Pigs, chickens, and sometimes the antique Chinese gentleman in a sedan chair carried by sweating coolies. And it's a pretty drive.

The tour picks up its people at their hotels. Drives out Kowloon's main street, Nathan Road, that crowded bazaar of watch shops, tailors, camera and transistor-radio dealers. (You'll want to walk this later.)

This goes on for several miles. The shops carry black Chinese characters on red banners (a lucky color). Somewhat frustrating since you can't read them. But the guide should tell you.

(One is for a soft drink—"Drink of a Thousand Delights." The British less poetically call it "Bubble Up.")

There's a stop at a rather grim-looking group of block buildings festooned with drying laundry. This is the Resettlement Estates. Chinese refugees, packed one family to the room.

Moving various squatters around is a constant problem of the British colonial government. Red China has intervened—and won—often enough in these affairs to chill British blood.

You can take photos here. But you'll be surrounded by kids all holding out a hand. You can carry small change. But passing it out only increases the number. I've found no way to handle it.

(In most countries, I carry a pocketful of balloons. Blow them up and give them to kids. But here the children outnumber you.)

There are more than 3000 factories along this way. Part of the Hong Kong urgency to take care of the overflowing worker population.

The road takes you into the rural valleys.

Women work the rice, wearing the black pajamas and fringed black hats of the farm people. You might notice that in planting, they don't squat but bend from the hips with legs straight.

The men plow with water buffaloes. And if you are there in harvest time, you see them beating the grain with ancient wooden flails.

You go through a walled native village. See the kitchen and bath facilities and take the usual pictures.

At the sign *Closed Area* on the road, you climb to a pine-topped hill and look toward the wandering Samchun River. Everything on the other side is Red China.

You return by a different route, passing a peasant market, shoreline docks with sampans and fishing junks.

Hong Kong Island Tour ($5–$8.75 by car or Minibus) Start from Kowloon and cross on the Vehicular Ferry. You drive to the Peak tram station for a ride up to the top of the peak on a funicular railway. It's an excellent view of the harbor, the ships and junks, the islands and mountains of the mainland beyond.

There are souvenir shops and restaurant-bars and you

have an English-speaking guide to tell you that Hong Kong means "fragrant waters." (Some other sources say it means "bad-smelling waters." But who's going to argue?)

On this route you see the Tiger Balm Gardens. A sort of Oriental fantasy of the late Ah Boon Haw, who invented Tiger Balm. You can get this all-purpose remedy in pills or in ointment to rub on for everything from sore throat to headache.

Chinese swear by it—I don't know the medical ingredients, but I suspect a lot of faith goes into it. Anyway, it made Ah Boon Haw a millionaire. And it built the gardens of statuary and flowers.

The tour then takes you by car along the Island Road to Tai Tam Tuk Reservoir and the village of Stanley. Lunch is served at the very British, very stylish Repulse Bay Hotel.

You eat on the veranda with a view of the islands and bay.

After lunch, you go to Deepwater Bay and Aberdeen fishing village—the shoreside connection of the Water People who live on the massed junks and sampans.

The rest of the drive is a prideful pointing out of universities and hospitals and residential sections. Time is four and a half hours, and tour covers 38 miles.

Launch Tour of the Harbor (about $7)
This takes you past the big ship-docking berths to the Typhoon Shelter. But if you pay $9, you can make this trip at night—which is much more satisfying.

At night, the fishing junks are back in their appointed places on the water streets.

Family life is going on behind the red curtains. The delicatessen boat is sculled up and down the waterways, the boatman calling out the wares he will bring, piping hot, to your gangway.

The floating mah jongg games are going. The sides of the boat are open to any passing viewer.

The singsong girls' boats are floating musically by, asking for customers who will pay them to stay and sing alongside.

There are water streets of "flower girls." Each girl in her own sampan, with soft lighting showing the quality of the interior furnishings.

This tour also includes dinner on one of the Aberdeen floating restaurant boats, which you should do in any case. The dinners are excellent.

There is a two-hour tour of the area in a launch if you have little time. I notice one of the sights now pointed out is listed as "the Suzie Wong Hotel." Thus fame comes to the rough, tough Wanchai dock district.

Evening Tour ($9)
This runs about four hours. A drive through Victoria City (the real name of what we call Hong Kong—Hong Kong is the island).

Usually you ride up the Peak to look at the lighted city and harbor. It's worth it. And if the day has been hot, the Peak is usually cooler. You drive through the native markets, always flaring with torchlights and lively with business. Noisy and gay and colorful.

This also takes you to Aberdeen, where you catch a sampan to the floating restaurant for dinner.

Homeward with a stop at the Chinese Opera. It's a little on the wailing side when the five-note Chinese scale hits Western ears. The audience eats watermelon seeds, spitting the husks casually on the floor.

(You eat popcorn and throw the bag on the floor. Now *there's* a curious custom.)

It's a lively, participating, chattery audience. The show goes on for hours and stagehands move the furniture around in the midst of the heroine's dying speeches.

You return at midnight to the very British Peninsula Hotel for a round of drinks.

Macao Tour ($27 for overnight trip and return)
Macao is the Portuguese colony famed for open sin, opium dens, firecrackers, and gambling.

I hear it has been somewhat cleaned up recently in the interests of tourism.

The wicked Central Hotel, where we used to let our bets down in wicker backets to the basement gambling rooms (the hotel was built around this central light well), is not gambling these days.

However, there's an old ferry tied up at the wharf where you can play *fan tan* and *pai gow*.

There are plans for two tourist hotels and a luxury gambling casino. Gambling is the big thing in Macao, and every Chinese is a horseplayer at heart.

You are picked up at your hotel at 10 P.M. and taken to the Macao steamer. A four-hour trip, leaving at 11:30.

The boat is comfortable. Nice enough cabins. You dock at three in the morning and sleep until eight. Breakfast on the boat or at the Villa Tai Yip hotel.

The architecture has the Portuguese flavor of the tiled-front fishing towns across the Tagus, south of Lisbon. Streets have fine shade trees. The houses are Mediterranean blues and pinks and yellows.

There are a number of fine Chinese temples here. And here, in 1844, the first treaty between the U.S. and China was signed.

You see the barrier gate where Chinese and Portuguese sentries stand face to face. (The Portuguese soldiers here are blacks from Mozambique.)

Touring of the residential sections. Plenty of gambling houses. Return by steamer in the afternoon.

This trip can be done on your own—$3.50 for the 40-mile ride to Macao by night and $1.50 for the return in the afternoon.

The Villa Tai Yip has 10 good rooms, a garden, and good food if you want to stay over.

You do need a temporary visa on your passport. The Portuguese consul at Hong Kong does this for about $3.

It's worth the trip for the town and the barrier gate where coffins are opened as they cross (for "live" refugee corpses). Country ducks are prodded. (They're sometimes stuffed with illegal gold.) All kinds of smuggling goes on—if you know someone to tell you where to look.

There are any number of local tour agencies where you can buy any of these tours. Most of them have desks in the major hotels.

AND ANOTHER THING

An excellent source for all kinds of information is Pan American Airways—offices in Hong Kong and in the

Peninsula Hotel in Kowloon. Most of the tour background here was produced by Robin Kinkead in Pan-Am's San Francisco public relations office. The line was the first air carrier to hook up Hong Kong and the U.S.

Every hotel desk has a number of thick, handsome shopping guides, filled with advertising. It's easy enough to find what you want through these. But whether you get the best price seems to be a matter of comparison.

There is no night-club tour that I have seen advertised or taken. I'd go to a few of the standard clubs—Maxim's is a good one. And I'd take in the Luk Kwok, the "Suzie Wong" hotel with the hilarious Chinese cowboy band.

The Wanchai dock area is for sailors and is rough.

The dance halls, while elegant, are for men. They don't want amateur competition brought in against the $11-an-hour (Hong Kong money) hostesses.

The native Chinese quarters can be visited safely at night. They're at their busiest, crowded and noisy. Some danger of getting your pocket picked or a handbag grabbed if you are careless. People are poor and you look rich.

Rickshaw riding always ends in an argument over price. And Al Kay of PanAm was badly hurt when a car crashed into one he was riding. I'm against them. Take a taxi.

Streets are well-policed by very tough Chinese on the colonial force. However, I avoid dark alleys and walking around after midnight except on the main roads.

If it's late at night or the Star Ferry isn't running, take a walla-walla boat. These little launches are at the waterfront where you come off the ferry. They run when they've got customers. $1 U.S. for the crossing.

THE PHILIPPINES

"Here Rests in Honored Glory
A Comrade in Arms
Known but to God."

Tired, footsore infantrymen of the 37th Division, their bones aching from almost continuous marching, have their hands full tonight. They are crouched behind corners of buildings on Manila's Rizal Avenue and are sighting their M-1s from behind pillars holding up the roofs of the city's Spanish type sidewalks in the downtown district. With months and months of New Georgia's and Bougainville's jungle warfare behind it, the 37th is tonight getting its first taste of street fighting. The dogfeet are in the heart of Manila, and death is staring at them from behind unfamiliar metropolitan objects.

—Sgt. Dick Hanley in Yank, *1945*

MONEY. Philippine peso $3.50-$3.85 to $1 U.S.—varies.

BEST TIME TO GO. November–February

LANGUAGE. Tagalog, the dialect of the Manila area, is the lingua franca of the islands. However, there are 87 main linguistic groups in the 7000-plus islands of the archipelago.

The older families speak Spanish—a status symbol to mark their pure descent from the conquerors.

The American occupation in 1898 brought English to the schools as an official language.

English is the newspaper-and-TV language, and gets you by. But you still find many people who don't speak it; they speak only their native dialect.

You pick up a few words of Tagalog (descendant, like others, of Malaysia and India, probably).

In speaking English, they use *p* and *f* interchangeably. I noticed during the war that "Filipino fighter pilot" often came out "Pilipino pighter pilot."

There's a lot of ritual and ritualistic words used in the back country. The variety of knives and their names and uses by the Moros—from ritual decapitation to castration of the enemy.

The Pacific pidgin never seems to have invaded these islands as it did all the others.

Manila is warm and tropical and exotic. The purple-and-gold sunsets fill the evening sky like a splash from a painter's palette. The evening brings the jasmine smell of the white sampaguita flower—cousin to the *tiare tahiti* and the Hawaiian *pikake*.

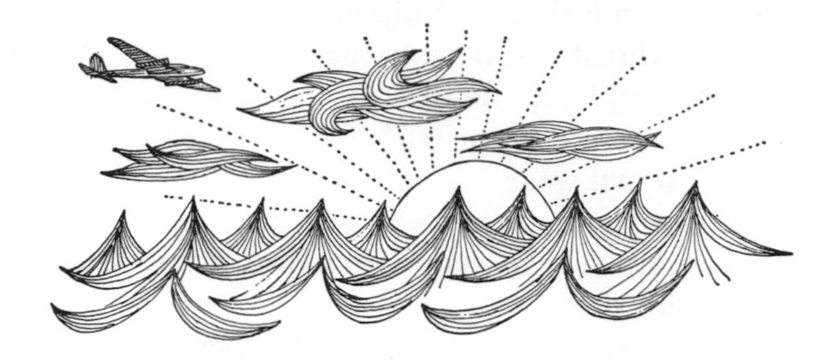

There is a rich odor of Philippine cigars. And the restaurants float their wares on the night—foods with wonderful names: *Nilagang karne at Manok, Pancit loglog, Paksiw na Bangos, Adobong Manok at Baboy.*

* * *

U.S. and Canadian citizens need a visa, and smallpox vaccination dated within the last three years, to get in by air where tall, green *cogon* grass lines the runways. Or by sea where a few sunken Japanese warships still raise a mast above the water.

The biggest tourist invasion was during the war. Thousands of Americans know the Philippines as a palm beach at Leyte. The splash of shells across the Pasig River, falling on the walls of the Spanish Intramuros fort. San Miguel beer drunk from a helmet on the road to Manila.

Customs is easy enough. Bring in a carton and a half of cigarettes. Philippine rum is excellent and San Miguel beer is known all over the Orient for its high quality.

You can drink water in Manila.

The weather at its best is usually muggy hot. (Hotels and night clubs are air-conditioned.)

Dress is tropical. The Filipinos wear a dress shirt, open at the throat and outside the pants. Called *barong tagalog.* I would get one of these right away. The embroidered ones are worn with tuxedo trousers and no jacket for formal wear.

Otherwise you have to wear coat and tie.

Filipinos are very formal, very polite. Every sentence is ended with *sir.*

They are also touchy and quick-tempered. Be polite and you'll have anything you want. Get impolite and you've got more trouble than you can handle.

* * *

I prefer the cool, tiled Manila Hotel with the long veranda and tropical garden. Across the street from the Luneta Park, where civic celebrations are held in front of the concrete reviewing stand.

A block away, where Dewey Boulevard begins its long curve along Manila Bay, is the Bay View. A few blocks further on is the Filipinas.

Both are good.

* * *

The city has a boom-boom night life. Dewey Boulevard is a string of clubs. They range from the elegant Cham-

pagne Room in the Manila Hotel to juke-box spots. *Balut* sellers in the front yard and chickens in the back.

The proprietor usually wears a war-surplus .45.

The clubs have hostesses to dance with. I must say most of them have an impersonal, dazed look—as though they'd been hit over the head with a club. It's like dancing with a store-window dummy.

The clubs are open at strange hours—a good many open at noon. Some stay open 24 hours. Taking on new shifts of hostesses and orchestras three times during the day.

Filipino orchestras are great. They have a real sense of music.

I would certainly take one morning—a good, hot Manila morning—to step into one of these dark, chilled night clubs and see the action.

Manila's night-club route also has a lot of "bini-boys." They wear long hair, dress like girls, work the boulevards, and can hit like a mule. In addition, most of them carry a razor-sharp equalizer called a *balisong.*

Most of my friends in Manila take taxis from club to club. (And hate me when I come out in print with this sort of thing.)

I've also done some sailors' hunting grounds—the Yellow Bar, the Merchant Marine, Kilroy's. But I don't advise it for the tourist.

* * *

Restaurants and food leave a lot to be desired. Prices are fairly stiff. Manila is a high-priced town.

The New Europe and the Swiss Inn were the best I found.

If you want to sample native food, *adobo* is one to try: chicken, pork, and beef with enough garlic to blow the door off a safe. *Sinigang* is stewed fish or meat with vegetables.

The *balut*, sold in little lantern-lit stands outside the night clubs, is a duck egg brought almost to hatching. Filipino playboys think highly of it as an aphrodisiac. Recipe: three *baluts* and two bottles of beer. You're in orbit.

Bibingka is a sort of midnight waffle. Rice and eggs (duck eggs buried in salt and mud), water-buffalo cheese. All this is made into a batter and baked with glowing charcoal top and bottom. When it comes out, it is sprinkled with sugar and curls of fresh coconut. Quite good.

* * *

Boy meets girl: Only in the hostess night clubs. Filipinas from good families go out chaperoned.

The hostesses, as I say, are pretty lethargic. Look away from the table for a moment, she pulls a napkin over her head and goes to sleep.

Some taxi drivers hustle you with pictures of girls. Each cabbie has his private string. It's rather dangerous. You can get slugged and rolled with no effort at all.

* * *

A small boat trip out to Corregidor is well worth while if you can make it.

The shell-scarred tunnels, the marks of war are there.

The marks of war are all over the Philippines. Downtown Manila is still rebuilding. This is where the Japanese dug in to die. About 20 per cent of the Manila Filipinos were killed in that frightful week.

* * *

Filipinos are wild gamblers. There is usually some illegal but open Las Vegas-style gambling spot.

You can bet on jai alai. Cockfighting is most popular. Your hotel will direct you.

* * *

The jeepney is the bus of Manila—a jeep remodeled into a six- or eight-passenger miniature bus.

"We have many sayings about the jeepney, sir," a driver told me.

"Like, 'A lady without a lover is like a jeepney without a driver.' "

The jeepney is painted with gorgeous, intricate designs. Blues, oranges, reds, greens.

They are the very personal property of the driver and carry names painted below the windshield: *Victory! Lazie Suzie. Coca-Cola. Balambang Baby.*

The *calesa* is a two-wheeled carriage drawn by a small horse.

The brass is highly polished. The *calesa* is brightly painted. Makes a nice sightseeing vehicle.

Taxis are not expensive. Plenty of them.

* * *

Philippine Air Lines flies into the major cities of the 7000 islands of the archipelago. You can also catch freighters out of Manila—Pacific Far East Lines of San Francisco has some excellent 12-passenger ships.

The outer islands are much more primitive.

Igorots who carve the wooden heads for tourists live northeast of Manila.

There are bow-and-arrow Negritos in the middle islands.

There are Mohammedan Moros in the big southern island of Mindanao.

Moros still sail their bright-sailed *vintas* up the coasts to raid Christian settlements and capture residents for slaves.

* * *

The Philippines have not had a great deal of tourist trade. You don't find many shops with tourist-type things. But a few are good buys.

Carved wooden salad bowls from the Igorot country are the best-looking I have seen.

The embroidered shirt, *barong tagalog,* for men is a dressy item at home for women. They make them in the smaller sizes. Philippine cigars ship well to friends at home.

There are a number of native fibers that weave wonderfully into cloth for evening gowns. *Piña,* made from pineapple plant fibers; *jusi,* made from raw silk and banana fiber; "Kinorus" hand-woven cotton from the Ilocos, comes in brightly colored stripes; *ramie* is machine-woven from a flaxlike weed. I've brought these home with great success.

* * *

A flight down to exotic Zamboanga is worth while. Moro country. The Davao Insular Hotel, in Davao is probably the most modern in the Philippines. You could try the durian fruit here. It doesn't smell very good. But the Maro *datus*—the chiefs—who marry 250 wives, say it keeps you feeling like a twenty-year-old.

In hot weather, try a break up at Baguio in the cooler mountains. This is a summer resort and has good hotels. You fly it in short time from Manila. It is on the same island of Luzon.

Tour services will take you around Manila. To the

presidential residence at Malacañang Palace. To Santo Tomas, the ancient university that was used as a civilian prisoner-of-war camp. To various falls and high-ridge views.

If you can get to Banaue, north of Baguio, you see rice paddies carved into mountainsides over many, many years. A big job of primitive engineering.

Have your driver take you just outside Manila to the American military cemetery—alongside where the old Philippine Scouts had their headquarters.

It is filled with graves of the ones who stayed behind, died on the death march from Bataan, never identified. Each marked with a stone cross:

Here Lies in Honored Glory,
A Comrade in Arms
Known but to God.

Manila Hotels

Manila Hotel: Overlooking Manila Bay. Swimming pool, tennis court, and golf course. There's an arcade of shops you might like. Air-conditioned. Across from the Luneta, the big public park. Tile floors, breezeways. This is my first choice.

Bay View: On Dewey Boulevard, also facing the bay. All air-conditioned. Pretty good.

Filipinas: Four or five blocks from the other two major hotels. On Dewey Boulevard, in the center of the night-club area. There's a view, a swimming pool, and a shopping arcade.

Manila Restaurants

New Europe: OK food. European menu. This restaurant's a favorite of Ken Macker, who runs the Philippines *Herald* and is a knowledgeable man on groceries abroad.

Sky Room, Jai Alai: Both American and Philippine food here. It's in the same building as the jai alai courts. A plenty exciting sport with much gambling going on.

Fish Fun: In the Malabon district. You sit in the middle of a fishpond and catch your own dinner. Cooked in Philippine style, but there are Continental items on the card too.

Bulakena: If you want to try Philippine specialties, this is the best choice. It's near the hotels.

Bamboo Room: In the Manila Hotel. Good Philippine dishes.

Luzon

Taal Vista Lodge, Tagaytay (subsidiary of Manila Hotel).

Baguio

Mount Data Lodge, Bontoc (new; subsidiary of Pines Hotel).

Pines Hotel: 144 rooms here, all with bath. Rates change with the seasons. Cheapest from June to November. Intermediate: December to February, Highest: March to May. Lots of sports activities, including golf.

Davao

Davao Insular Hotel: 104 air-conditioned rooms. Swim in the ocean or in the pool. Water skiing, boating, skin diving. Golf. Eight shops in the arcade. Most modern in the Philippines.

Zamboanga

Hotel Bayot by the Sea: 61 rooms with bath and some air conditioning. This has swimming in the ocean, a bar, dining on the terrace, and a souvenir shop. Golf course 2½ miles away.

HOW TO GET THERE

Airlines: Air France, BOAC, Cathay Pacific, Civil Air Transport, Pan American, Northwest Orient Airlines, Philippine Air Lines.

Steamship Lines: American Mail Line, American President Lines, Java Pacific & Hoeg Lines, Pacific Far East Lines, P & O–Orient Lines, Royal Interocean Lines.

TO READ ALONG THE WAY

Bare Feet in the Palace by Agnes Newton Keith, *The Philippines—Young Republic On the Move* by D. Van Nostrand, *Land of The Morning* by Delores Stevenson.

When you arrive, read the Philippines *Herald*. It's in English.

FOR MORE INFORMATION. PATA, 442 Post Street, San Francisco. Your carrier. And there are Philippine consulates in New York City at 350 Fifth Avenue; in Washington, D.C., at 1617 Massachusetts Avenue, N.W.; in Chicago at 201 N. Wells; in Los Angeles at 448 South Hill Street; in New Orleans at 611 Gravier; in San Francisco at the World Trade center in the Ferry Building; and in Seattle at 1741 Smith Tower.

Philippine Travel Information offices are located in New York and San Francisco.

Tours

There are some real adventure tours of the Philippines. There are more than 7000 islands in the archipelago—some 4000 are not even named.

There are tribesmen so wild that they still use bows and arrows.

There are tribesmen who must take a human head before they have proved the manliness needed to get married.

The American Army .45-caliber pistol became part of

our weapons here. It was the only hand gun powerful enough to stop a Moro gone *juramentado*—the religious wholesale killing of Christians by which a Moslem is lifted bodily to heaven.

There are peculiar marriage customs dating to some dim time when the first Moro *vintas* sailed into these islands.

* * *

Not all of these are available on tours. But you can get close enough to smell the flavor. The country towns with names like a gong beating: Bongabong and Tagaytay, Dipolog, Zamboanga, Dinagat, Panay, Palawan, Balabac and Bulacan. Iloilo, Camarines Sur, Pampanga, and Misamis Oriental.

There is a volcano called Hibok-Hibok. And footpads use a lethal belt knife called a *balisong*.

Up in the hills near Baguio, the primitive Igorots carve hardwood and eat dog as a delicacy.

On lush Mindoro, there are a few Japanese soldiers. Waiting for the Emperor's fleets to rescue them. Not knowing that the war is long over.

Magellan was killed on the island of Mactan.

The islands are bombarded with tropical rains. And the sunsets are splashes of the most vivid colors ever seen.

It is not a particularly comfortable land for the traveler. But it is rewarding. Much of the value is what imagination tells you lies just beyond the line of sight.

Manila Tour ($25 for one day and night)
You are met at the airport and transferred to a first-class air-conditioned hotel.

Afternoon is sightseeing. Manila is a rather pretty tropical city.

It's unlikely that a regular tour will take you through native sections—we all like to show off our millionaire homes. But if you have a private driver, you could ask for it.

Manila has grown increasing numbers of slums as country folk crowded in after the war. But there are some districts of grassy *nipa* huts. Washing hanging on the line and chickens under the slat floors built above flooding rain level.

The tour will show you Malacañang Palace, home of the President. The Luneta, Manila's park and official parade ground, lies across from the Manila Hotel.

The Intramuros was the original Spanish walled city. American shells destroyed it during the terrible fighting for Manila. Squatters live in the caverns of the walls. There are standing church walls and parts of the old Fort Santiago where American prisoners were held under torturous conditions.

Santo Tomas University was founded in 1611. It was a civilian concentration camp during the Japanese occupation.

You see the University of the Philippines. The Rizal sports stadium. And certainly you will be taken to Forbes Park, "millionaire village."

More impressive to me is the nearby U.S. Military Cemetery. The long, orderly rows of 17,000 white crosses, the flags flying overhead, and the monotonous regularity of the unknown—and 19,000 names of men missing in action listed on the walls of a single monument.

There are launches running out to Corregidor Island that guards the harbor. The price seems to vary. About $15.

When I went there, the famed Malinta tunnel was closed. Still dangerous by reason of undiscovered booby traps. I have since heard that you can now enter up to a point.

This was the American headquarters and hospital and last stand.

Baguio Tour ($33 for two days and one night)
A favorite week-end spot for people from Manila. Baguio is up in the cool hills and affords a fine place to get away from Manila's constant tropical heat.

You fly up and have a choice of coming back by plane or train. I'd recommend the train. It gives you a look at the countryside—a long vista of rice paddies shimmering green.

The Filipino lives on rice. And this is the major rice bowl.

If it is planting season, a guitar player (hired by the planting crew) follows the planters. It's stooping, back-breaking labor. And the rice planter works better to the rhythm of the guitar.

Most of the Philippine rice trade is a national scandal.

The sharecropping planter gets little return—about 10 per cent of the crop has been the usual ratio.

"I could stop every political revolt in the Philippines by giving the rice worker twenty per cent of what he raises," a Filipino ambassador told me once.

The favorite rice workers' song has a ring of misery:

> Planting rice is no fun,
> All must work till the day is done.
> Cannot rest, cannot sit,
> Cannot rest for a little bit.

There's a day of sightseeing around the pine hills of Baguio on arrival. You stay at the Pines Hotel, one of the best.

This is primitive Igorot country and you should see some of these countrymen. The women are often bare-breasted and the men wear loincloths.

Their hardwood carvings are excellent. The wooden heads are sculptured works.

An excellent buy: Look for the enormous carved salad bowl with the little dressing bowl carved right onto it. There are also small serving bowls to go with the larger one. Mine was inexpensive, useful when I got home, and causes a lot of envy. What else do we travel for?

Tagaytay Tour ($12 for the day)
Another Manila favorite. You go by private car. Lunch at Taal Vista Lodge—a marvelous view. Visit Las Piñas

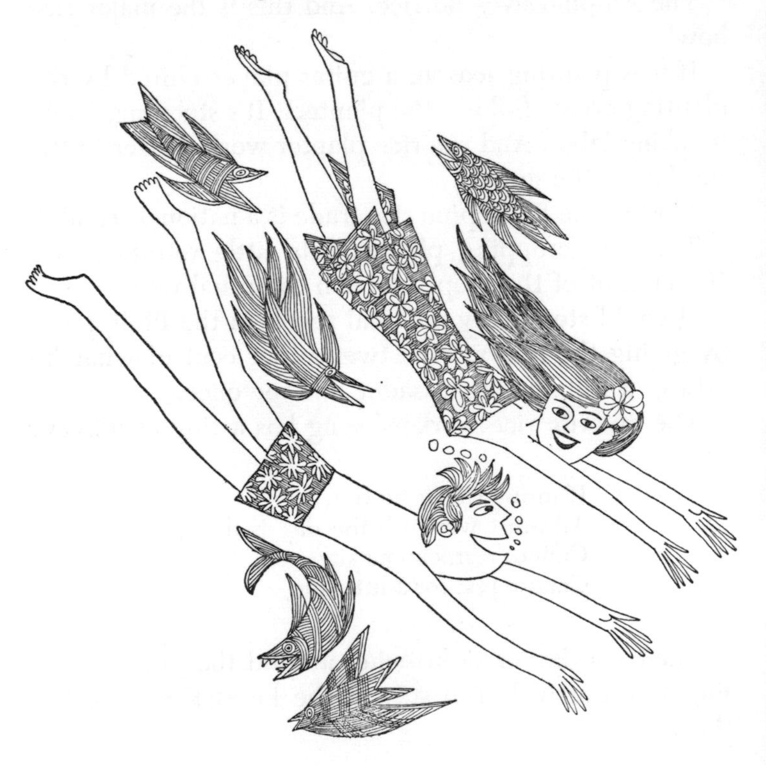

and see the famous bamboo organ. Return to Manila.

You can stay overnight at Taal Vista Lodge for $5.50 if you like. It's cool, if you find Manila heat getting to you.

Pagsanjan Falls Tour ($34 for the day and overnight in Manila)

This is with private car and driver-guide. Out Dewey Boulevard along the bay and through the rice fields and coconut plantations—a very good picture of rural life.

The big thing of this tour is the ride down the rapids through deep gorges to Pagsanjan Falls.

Not as interesting to me as the ride through the countryside. But great if you like to ride rapids.

Hundred Islands Tour ($45 for three days)

An all-included cost by motor coach ($60 by private car) to the best beach resort in the Philippines. Plenty of fishing, skindiving and all the personal private beaches you want.

You can combine this trip with Baguio nicely.

Zamboanga Tour

This is the Moro country and certainly worth seeing. It was the first area fortified by the Spaniards. Seldom visited by the casual traveler—the southernmost part of the islands. It has an unspoiled charm hard to find elsewhere.

The Moro *vinta* is a hollowed-out log. With a bamboo outrigger and colored sails as gay as the sunsets. You see them at the villages on stilts. The colorful dress of the Moro is a regular sight on the streets.

The *vinta* sailors fish and pearl-dive and sometimes raid the northern islands for Christian slaves.

A few high-powered chiefs have hooked high-powered motors onto their *vintas* and run every kind of contraband from cigarettes to guns.

The best of souvenirs here are black coral and pearls. And the handmade Moro knives. These are so ceremonial that there are a couple of dozen, each with its task.

A knife has been invented for every unkind cut known to man. There's one bound in two halves of bamboo lashed with vines. It is not drawn from the scabbard. The user simply hits the opposition across the neck—*whack!*

The knife cuts through the lashings and the two halves of bamboo fall off. It's the original quick-draw.

Bayot Hotel on the bay is your best. The rate is about $6.

Cebu City

This is the oldest city in the Republic. The gold image of the Holy Child in San Augustin Church is supposed to have come with Magellan in 1521.

There is a cross planted by Magellan. And a monument to Lapu-Lapu, the Mactan island chief who stuck the Portuguese explorer with a sharp spear. Thus ending his voyage around the world.

The new Magellan is your hotel here. About $8.

Davao Tour

On Mindanao in an area thick with pineapple. Davao is the modern, major city of the southern island.

It's now popular for the modern Davao Insular Hotel. Similar to the big tourist hotels of Waikiki Beach. All the regular sports—golf, horseback riding, skindiving, water sports, and indoor martinis. About $4 per night.

Lot of very pretty Moro girls with unusually thick black hair.

If you can only go one place, though, take Zamboanga.

All tours can be bought in the islands. But you might like to make advance reservations through Philippine Air Lines, whose jets fly the Pacific.

Internally, you fly PAL throughout all the islands.

Or you can loaf at sea on the ships of Compañia Maritima and the Philippine Steam Navigation Company.

The highway system is very good on the island of Luzon. But if you hire a car, make some local inquiries.

The Americans and Japanese left a lot of guns loose in the country.

Thousands of Filipinos learned every guerrilla trick from blowing a dam to assassinating the passing motorist. Some areas are dangerous at certain times.

Same goes for night-life tours. There are several—about $16.

You can do it alone. But you ought to have a local friend. Some of the places have some rough characters.

MALAYSIA

"The day English soldiers swept the streets, Singapore was lost to Great Britain forever," said a British resident.

On the day after all his things had been put on board the ship, he sent for me and I went to the room where he used to write. He said, "Take this letter and keep it carefully, with the one I gave you at Malacca. If hereafter any distinguished Englishman comes here, show him the letters and he will befriend you. Moreover, should you get work in the Court, show the letters to whoever is then at the head of affairs in Singapore, and you will receive a higher salary than is usually paid to Malays. Do not grieve, for if I live I will surely return to Singapore; but should I die, then goodbye, and I charge you to diligently learn the English language until you know it well. Here is another paper; take it and when I have gone give it to Mr. Queiros, who will pay you two hundred dollars, which I ask you to accept from me. If I ever return, I want to write several books dealing with the countries in this neighborhood; in them I will mention your name and the great help you have given me in all Malay matters and everything that was within your knowledge, so that white men may know you and trust you." I could not speak, but took the papers while the tears streamed down my face without my being conscious of it. That day, to part with Sir Stamford Raffles was to me as the death of my parents.

–from an account by Abdullah, son of Abdulkadir, of Raffles' final departure from Singapore in June 1823

MONEY. Malaya dollars (written with the $ sign); $1 U.S. equals $3.03.

BEST TIME TO GO. Weather is almost constantly tropical. Average of 15 days of rain a month. Midday runs 88 degrees, temperature never falls lower than 73 degrees.

LANGUAGE. English, Malay, and a lot of Chinese.

Singapore

This is a pretty, tropical island lying close to the tip of the Malay Peninsula. Operated as a self-governing member of the British Commonwealth, but it hooked up with Malaysia in 1963.

Since the British ran Singapore for years, its lush tropical growth has a barbered look about it. The streets are lined with flaming flamboyant. But the vines are carefully cut back and trimmed.

In the breezeway Raffles Hotel bar at evening, everybody is in white shorts with knee-high socks. Dinner is lightly formal.

If you want to be cool, have one of the Indian tailors run you up a quick bush jacket and slacks—they pattern them after those worn by Indonesian army officers.

This gives you a short-sleeve jacket. No shirt. No tie. But it's accepted dinner wear. Otherwise you're in coat and tie. No aloha shirts in the evening. Bush jackets and slacks (if you get them with shorts you have to wear knee-length socks) should run about $10 in khaki—for day. About $15 in white linen—for night.

* * *

You can drink the water. Medical and drugstore operation like that in Great Britain.

I'd be careful about eating at any street stands. There are some wonderful, strange tropical fruits here I've never seen before. But eat them from the hotel kitchen.

Your hotel will probably be the famed Raffles.

But the next time I am in Singapore, I'm going to stay at the Cockpit. It looked even better to me. An old, restored mansion where you arrive under a stately white portico.

A very lively bar. Saturday and Sunday is the big Java *rijsttafel* day.

This is a bed of rice on which you put about 40 different spicy meats, chicken, fish, and various condiments.

It is served traditionally: Four Malays in turbans, jackets, and wraparounds carry it around. I've had it in Curaçao, in Amsterdam, and in Manila. This is easily the best of them all.

This is served late noonish—1:30 is a good time. And make reservations.

* * *

Local customs: No problem at the airport. Change some money into Malaya dollars at the airport bank.

Malays go very big for etiquette. Team this up with British reserve among the British working here and you've got a formal town.

You might remember Malays do not shake hands. (You can put your palms together in front of your forehead and bow slightly. This goes well all over the southern parts of the Far East.)

Malays handle food only with the right hand.

It is not good form to show emotion. The belly laugh is out.

Tipping is 10 per cent.

* * *

Singapore has some million people, more than three-fourths of them Chinese.

Plenty of Chinese restaurants.

Plenty of Malay and Indian curries. Barbecued lamb is a favorite you'll see on menus under the name *satay*.

Among the restaurants European style: The grill in the Cockpit Hotel; the Elizabethan Grill in the Raffles; the Cathay restaurant on top of the Cathay building.

Prince's on Orchard Road has music and dancing and the food was good.

The Adelphi Grill in the Adelphi Hotel was good.

Breakfast is in the English style—kippers, 10 kinds of marmalade, and frightful coffee. (But you can ask for Nescafé.) You can also get early-morning tea if you dig that sort of thing.

I do. I got whipped into morning tea in Fiji at the Grand Pacific Hotel.

The Wentworth Hotel in Sydney continued it—I couldn't get them to shut off the blasted stuff. The management got huffy and said since I'd ordered it one morning, by heaven, I'd get it *every* morning. Otherwise it made too much work for the staff, changing my mind all the time.

By and by, I got hooked on it.

* * *

This is a free port—no duty, no taxes. It seemed to me that a number of things were cheaper than in the free port of Hong Kong. I priced out a Minox camera at $80 U.S. compared to $110 in Hong Kong.

There was a good selection of Japanese and German cameras.

Good selection of Japanese binoculars and transistor radios.

Good choice of Indian saris and Thai silks. And the

dressmaking prices were very, very good. Tailoring I had done was a little on the British side. Short in the coat length.

But Singapore cannot compare with Hong Kong's profusion of things to buy.

The shops are not as glistening. The shopping area has a run-down, battered look to it. (But this is Chinese tradition. Chinese don't like to buy in a chrome-and-glass place. They figure, rightly, that somewhere all the glitter is tacked on the price.)

Anything in tropical wear is good. Shorts, shirts with short sleeves, daytime dresses, bush jackets.

Tip: When they make pants for you, tell them to give you a half-inch or more of belt loop. They made mine just big enough to run a kite string through.

You can buy carved Bali heads and Malayan silverware. Star sapphires and jade—but you'd better know your stones. Thai silk if you aren't going on to Bangkok. You can get Thai silk in Hong Kong. But a lot of it there comes from Red China, so get a Certificate of Origin. U.S. Customs at Honolulu are very suspicious when you come back through.

* * *

Boy meets girl: Only by chance. There are taxi dancers in the three big amusement parks—The Happy World, The Great World, and The New World.

You pay an admission ticket and wander around among sideshows and shooting galleries.

My room boy thought this was the greatest pleasure in life. Not me.

One interesting thing: At the taxi dance, when the girls are *not* dancing with anyone, they stand in front of your table and do a sort of twist. All by themselves. I guess to prove they are in working action.

* * *

As it is all over the Far East, the day of the pukka sahib and the White Man's Burden is going out fast. May be out altogether.

When the Japanese took this British fortress, they put the British soldiers to work sweeping the streets. The lowliest coolie job.

The Malays and Chinese watched this.

Things have never been the same since.

Penang and Kuala Lumpur

These are one-day stopovers on the way to or from Bangkok. Colorful enough Malay towns with good hotels, and good swimming at Penang.

You fly this on Malayan Airlines. But I'd recommend the all-day trip by excellent train between Singapore and Kuala Lumpur or Kuala Lumpur and Penang. Good food. Good service. And you see the countryside, which is tropical and colorful.

Bangkok

The language is Thai—and believe me that's about all. It belongs to the Siamese-Chinese language group known as Tai. Each syllable has five identifying tones.

The language comes from original, ancient Siamese, which was monosyllabic with five tones to each syllable. There are about 15,000 words in the language of today's use. Spoken by 20,000,000 Thailanders.

The original Siamese merged somewhat with the language in which the sacred books of Buddha were written—the language of the Kingdom of Magadha. Hard town to get around in as the taxi drivers work only in Thai. Plus about 10 different and rising prices.

The money is the Thai baht, broken down into 100 satangs—21 baht to $1 U.S.

You legally bring in five packages of cigarettes. But the Customs people didn't blink at two cartons in my baggage.

You need a passport but no visa for visits up to 90 days.

* * *

I stayed at the American-favored Erawan. But the Oriental, with a view of the river, looked good to me.

The thing to do here is to see the various temples.

Bangkok is a holy city and there are a number of them. Richly ornamented and heavily incensed. (Or else somebody was cooking lunch next door.)

The tourist bureaus push sightseeing. Most people take trips around the interlacing canals, called *klongs.* And go see the Royal Palace and the Royal Barges.

The tourist bureau has an interesting exhibit of native handicrafts. You can buy them in the building.

There is a good English-language newspaper, *The Bangkok World.*

No legal gambling. But it's largely a Chinese town. Again, like the Chinese shops of Singapore, the merchants have deliberately gone for a rundown look. So the city downtown has a frame-shack sort of appearance.

Dress is lightweight tropical.

Temperatures run in the 90s year round. It there's a good time to go, it would be December through February. From June to October is monsoon season, with heavy rains more than half the month.

An umbrella is better than a raincoat in any of these countries. It can double as a sunshade. A raincoat roasts you.

The best taxis are the little cars on back of a motorcycle. They have a fringed awning. They're open and breezy. They're cheap.

* * *

Don't drink the tap water. Tipping is 10 per cent. The hotels add a 20-per-cent tax *and* a 10-per-cent service charge. I didn't find it inexpensive.

Liquor is high and lunches were a fair clip.

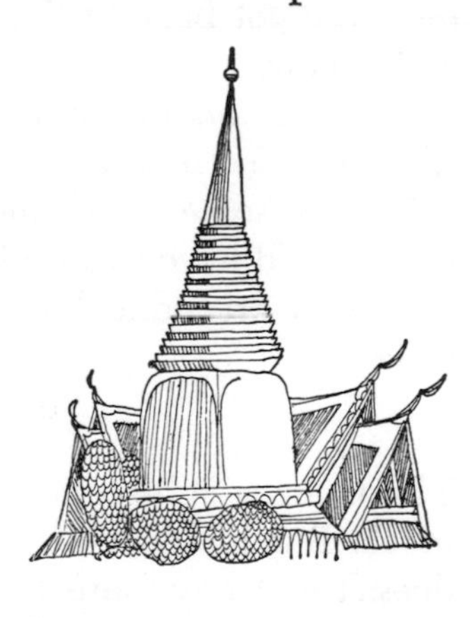

The Erawan food was good. I ate several times at the Skyroof Restaurant of the Oriental Hotel just for the view. The food was good and they made a fair enough dry martini.

Generally, though, I'd stick with the Singapore sling or Pimm's Cup which are well-known and well-made all over this area. French wine was expensive.

* * *

Boy meet girl: Tourist girls may get dancing at the Erawan. Boys at the Lido, the L–85, the Luna Club, the Sani Chat Cay, the Chez Eve, and the Champagne Room. All with hostesses.

The clubs didn't have much glitter. But the music was pretty good.

* * *

Thai silks are the big thing to buy here. There are also jewelry stores with star sapphires and antique jewelry. Quite a bit of jingle-bell Oriental costume jewelry. Didn't look to me like it would be wearable once you got back in the U.S. Unless you are working a sideshow.

Lots and *lots* of Neilloware—the oxidized and inlaid silver you see now in tourist shops all over the world.

There's some brass-and-horn tableware that looks good. You'd have to ship it.

Lots of crocodile bags, snakeskin shoes, belts, and wallets.

* * *

This being a sightseeing town, I didn't get with it very much. But it's on your round-the-Pacific route and it doesn't cost any more to stop.

I got taken day after day by taxi drivers. Tip the doorman and find out exactly what it's going to cost you before you get in.

Angkor Wat

The flight out of Bangkok to the famous ruins is sometimes closed down by fighting troubles in Southeast Asia. But you can still get in from Phnom Penh in Cambodia, a very French colonial town way off the beaten tourist route.

Lunch and guides. Fix this with a travel agent before you leave the U.S.

Singapore Hotels

Raffles. The famous, imposing landmark of Singapore. The entrance is a circular drive along palm-shaded gardens. Yellow awnings flash in the sun. And the lobby looks like MGM's exotic East. Sit in the bamboo chairs around a bamboo table and order a Singapore sling. Just like Humphrey Bogart. The dining room is rather quiet in the mornings. And warm. Electric fans keep the air moving, but not much. Your room is actually a suite. With an outside writing room. The bedroom will be air-conditioned. And a dressing room and bath in the English style. Expensive.

Goodwood Park. Another imposing building, with a neon signature over the entrance. And a lot of blue mosaic tile. It looms high on a sloping hill in a good residential part of the city. Two stories high, with good, modern, large rooms. Many look out on the swimming pool. Expensive.

Adelphi. In the center of the business area. The hotel is old and tropical, the lobby is small, but the prices are not. Most European languages spoken. Air-conditioned.

Cathay. Has 140 air-conditioned rooms. Floor shows, dancing, movies, and a hairdresser. High prices.

Sea View. In a happy water's-edge location a half-hour drive from the center of town. Lots of beach and palm trees. Moderate prices.

Ocean Park. Dining, dancing, golf, badminton. Air conditioning. Children's playground and two bars for adults. Moderate prices.

Cockpit. A redone old mansion. Great. Cute bars. Lots of lunch and dinner action. Moderate prices.

Singapore Restaurants

Elizabethan Grill in the Raffles. Wooden-beamed and paneled walls in the Tudor style. Wonderful roast beef, served with a flourish. Dinner hour is around 9 P.M. All the food is good here. But have roast beef.

Adelphi Grill. Best known for business lunches. The food is fine. Try chicken Kiev here. There's an orchestra playing classical and semiclassical music. Luxurious.

Cockpit Hotel Grill Room & French Restaurant. Excellent. Java *rijsttafel* is the Saturday and Sunday special. Served by costumed locals. Reservations suggested.

Prince's Restaurant. In a residential area. Dinner and dancing. Very popular. Food is excellent. Looks a lot like a Stateside restaurant and bar.

TO READ ALONG THE WAY

The Hostile Sun by T. Stacey, *Getting to Know Malaya* by Jim Breatveld, *Island of the East Indies* by Hawthorn Daniel, *The Malays, a Cultural History* by Sir Richard Winstedt.

ELECTRICAL CURRENT. Forget it. 230 volts, both AC and DC. Eighteen different types of plugs in use, depending upon the Chinese contractor involved.

HOW TO GET THERE

Airlines: Air India, BOAC, Cathay Pacific, Japan Air Lines, KLM Royal Dutch, Malayan Airways, Pan American, Qantas, TAI, Thai Airways.

Steamship Lines: American Mail Line, American President Lines, Java Pacific & Hoegh Lines, P & O–Orient Lines, Royal Interocean Lines, Union Steamship Co. of New Zealand.

FOR MORE INFORMATION

Pacific Area Travel Association, 442 Post Street, San Francisco. And your carrier.

Penang Hotels

Eastern & Oriental. Old British Victorian. The vast lobby filled with overstuffed furniture. Rooms are large, more like suites. Separate writing room. Morning tea with fresh pineapple and bananas comes up to your room every morning. Best part of the hotel is the promenade, which has a view of the Penang Straits toward mainland Malaya. White-sand beach. Flowering shrubs and high palms. A cannon pointed out to sea. A good place to sit on the seawall and relax.

Lone Pine. Several miles from Penang. Ten to be exact. Great beach. Small cabins available.

Penang Hill. Very modern. Perched on a hill. You get there by funicular railway. Nice gardens. Spectacular views of the mainland and the city of Georgetown. One of the highest points on the island.

Not much restaurant action here. My choice is the grill room of the Eastern & Oriental. English pub style. Plain food. I was told an Oriental restaurant will be built in the new 140-room addition.

Kuala Lumpur Hotels

Merlin. All 217 rooms have bath and air conditioning. Elfin Room, Chinese restaurant, Harlequin restaurant for Western tastes. Bamboo bar and a night club for dancing. Golf a mile away.

Federal. Also air-conditioned; 24-hour pushbutton room service. Mandarin Palace for Chinese and European food. Two dining rooms, three bars. A night club and a fair arcade of shops.

HOW TO GET THERE

Maylayan Airlines from Singapore or Bangkok. Also by rail from Bangkok. P & O–Orient floats in on regular schedules.

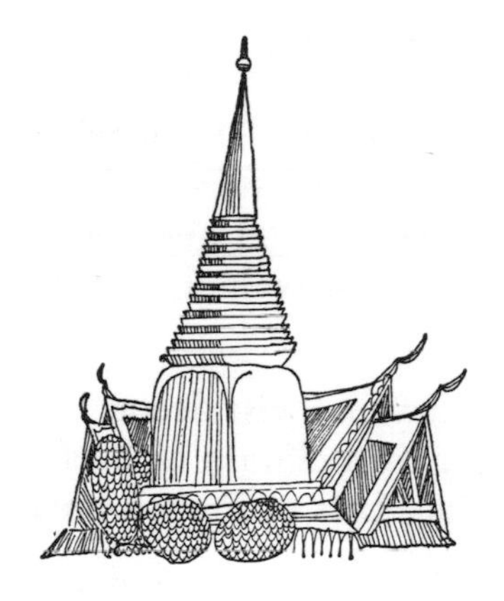

Thailand Hotels

Oriental. In the downtown area. New wing is very modern and rooms are air-conditioned. View of the Chao Phraya River. The bedrooms are split level. Sitting room on the lower level. Bedroom and bath on the higher floor. Separated by a draw curtain. Forget the old wing. Barrackslike rooms. Dining room is an open-air pavilion on the river side by the pool. Fountain and fishpond in open-air lobby. Prices high, but you get breakfast.

Erawan. Modern hotel. Lots of good ground around it. A few miles from downtown. The pool is just off the lobby. And most of the rooms have balconies with a pool view. The lobby has an elevated area with lounging chairs. To check the passing action. High prices. Classic Thai dances evenings. Tennis and golf.

Rama. Modern Oriental. Even the lobby is air-conditioned. More high prices. Thai dances several nights a week. Tropicana night club and three bars. Swimming pool and a good arcade of 24 shops. They speak French and German if you do.

King's Hotel. Bangkok's newest. Haven't seen it.

Bangkok Restaurants

Ambassador Club. In the Erawan Hotel. This is where you'll see the Thai classical dances. Western-style entertainment too. The show is good. Food and service fine. Dinner about U.S. prices. Drinks higher. Wine higher still.

Le Chalet Swiss. Also in the Erawan. Swiss decor. Fondue bourguignonne. Cook your own chunks of beef in the pot. Good with beer or wine. Lots of French bread and salad.

Normandy Grill. On the top floor of the Oriental Hotel. Nice view of the river. Continental food. Good steaks.

Or the Salinee. Or Nick's Place.

TO READ ALONG THE WAY

Read *Anna and the King of Siam.*

Be sure to see Thai boxing.

This is the halfway point on a Pacific trip. You can go home north or south from here. Same price.

Bangkok Tours

City Tour (about $8)
This tour by motor coach or car takes you to Lumpinee Park, near the Erawan Hotel and the Grand Palace. It's definitely a tour of the right district of town. The tree-shaded park, the tree-lined boulevard where the embassies are housed, the former palace of the King, now used as the National Assembly building. The big square is often used as a parade ground.

Continues to the Pasteur Institute. Big thing here of milking venom from poisonous snakes.

Onward to Nakorn Kasem, the Thieves' Market. This is the center for most of the silver and gold shops and, if you take the first asking price, it is rightly named. Siamese bronze and brassware and Thai silks in the shops, too.

Temple Tour (about $8)
Bangkok is the holy Buddhist city. You'll see plenty of priests on the streets—the men with shaved heads wearing a saffron-yellow toga sort of thing.

The gold-and-porcelain spires rise above what is one of the dingiest cities in the Orient. The downtown area is mostly shacky, wooden Chinese stores. But the temples are jeweled monuments in this clutter.

The Temple of the Reclining Buddha is a great complex of temple buildings. The Buddha is 160 feet in length, covered with gold leaf except for the soles of the feet, which are mother-of-pearl.

The Standing Buddha is of more modern appearance. It stands alone in a small park.

The Wat Trai Mitr or Golden Buddha is actually five and a half tons of gold.

The Marble Temple belongs to the Buddhist monastery. It is located in a garden surrounded by groves of shade trees. Built of marble imported from Italy, it contains another Buddha of great value and has Persian rugs on the floors.

The roof is typically Thai. The roof and doorways are edged in gold leaf matching the saffron robes of the monks you see in the gardens.

Palace Tour (about $9)
Takes you to three of the main palace buildings, but outer buildings and the complex of gardens is off limits. The main building can only be seen from the outside and looks more British Victorian than Thai.

The two flanking buildings are pure Thai—marble, gold leaf, mother-of-pearl. One is the King's funeral hall, the interior done in marble with heavy velvet draperies, painted murals and gold leaf. Next to it is the coronation hall, almost a duplicate of the funeral hall.

This tour continues to the Temple of the Emerald Buddha, the King's personal chapel, still within the palace compound. The gates are watched over by intricately carved demons and the temple is actually several buildings. Around the compound are murals of religious scenes from the life of Buddha and the temple door is inlaid with mother-of-pearl.

The Emerald Buddha is atop the gold-leaf altar with smaller gold-leaf Buddhas alongside. It is carved from a single piece of jasper.

In the compound is a model of the ruined city of Angkor Wat.

Klongs Tour (about $12.50)
By launch through the canals (*klongs*) to the Chao Phraya River takes you into luxuriant forests with small water-paths leading to the farms which feed the city.

The market is usually seen at yawning dawn if you want really to see the action. Most of the buying and selling is over at sunup.

There are some permanent markets on stilts. But most of it is done from the small boatside. Pretty colorful and pretty unsanitary looking. Everything goes into the water and everything comes out of it–including the drinking water, which is put into gigantic water jugs.

You also get a look at the King's barges with the golden-dragon heads.

Thai Boxing (about $13)
A lot of music, most of it Western. The difference seems to be that you can kick your opponent almost any place you can reach as well as belt him with regulation boxing gloves.

Thai Dancing (about $12)
Should do this one. (Dances regularly at the Erawan Hotel but they're kind of touristy.)

The dances are of antique origin and the costumes are historic. Swords, drums beating, much gold in the dress, and usually an interpreter to explain the meaning and background of the dance.

Nakorn Pathom Tour (about $15)
A 35-mile drive through rural scenery. Rice and old farmhouses. The first and oldest pagoda in Thailand is at Nakorn Pathom. It dates from 150 B.C.

Ayudhya Tour (about $25; full day, lunch included)
A drive 55 miles north. Ayudhya is the ancient capital of Thailand (1350–1767). It is now a city of historic ruins, somewhat restored by archeological digging. You stop on the return trip at Bang Pa Inn, the old royal summer palace within which is a Chinese palace—a gift from Chinese merchants during the reign of King Rama IV.

AND ANOTHER THING

The Bangkok–Penang Express is for the traveler looking for colorful countrysides, a train full of Thais, Malays, chickens, and livestock. Leaves Bangkok in the afternoon for a 700-mile run that ends 29 hours later when you board a ferry for the island of Penang.

Two first-class sleeping cars, vintage 1906 England.

Food is good—both Thai and Malay (some Western).

A pair of elephants named Frank and Jesse hold up the train regularly for handouts. Something like the bears in Yellowstone Park.

The train is not air-conditioned. Might be pretty hot in the warmer months.

AUSTRALIA

"He had a loose throat, Joe Barca did."

When we came to the place where the people were assembled, they all ran away; However we landed and leaving four boys to take care of the yawl, we walked up to some huts which were about two or three hundred yards from the waterside. When we had got some distance from the boat, four men, armed with long lances, rushed out of the woods, and running up to attack the boat, would certainly have cut her off, if the people in the pinnace had not discovered them, and called to the boys to drop down the stream; the boys instantly obeyed, but being closely pursued by the Indians, the cockswain of the pinnace, who was in charge of the boats, fired a musket over their heads; but of this they took no notice; and one of them lifting up his spear to dart it at the boat, another piece was fired which shot him dead. When he fell, the other three stood motionless for some minutes, as if petrified with astonishment; as soon as they recovered they went back dragging after them the dead body, which, however, they soon left, that it might not encumber their flight.

At the report of the first musket, we drew together, having straggled to a little distance from one another, and made the best of our way back to the boat; and crossing the river we soon saw the Indian lying dead upon the ground. Upon examining the body, we found that he had been shot through the heart; he was a man of middle size stature; his complexion was brown, but not very dark, and one side of his face was tattooed in spiral lines of a very regular figure; he was covered with a fine cloth, of a manufacture altogether new to us, and it was tied on exactly according to the representation in Valentyn's Account of Abel Tasman's Voyage, vol.

III., part 2, page 50: his hair also was tied in a knot on the top of his head, but had no feather in it. We returned immediately to the ship, where we could hear the people on shore talking with great earnestness, and in a very loud tone, probably about what had happened, and what should be done.

—from Captain James Cook's journal description of Terra Australis Incognita, first voyage; October 1769

MONEY. Australian pounds (2.24 to $1 U.S.)

BEST TIME TO GO. Spring (September, October, November), fall (March, April, May)

LANGUAGE. There's little chance you will learn or even hear any of the language used by Australia's Stone-Age aborigines (about 50,000, split into 600 tribal groups.) The "abo" talk has no relationship to any other known language. Abos working on farms generally speak in an English pidgin.

Walkabout is abo pidgin for an unexplained migratory urge which comes over the tame aborigine at certain times of the year. When he tells the sheep farmer "I go walkabout," he takes off for several months of apparently aimless wandering. Sometimes with the tribes, sometimes not. After that he returns, the feeling satisfied.

Australian English is colored with rhyming slang—a matter of much touchiness among the upper classes, since it was originally a prison slang brought in by the first transported criminals.

In all, England sent out some 60,000 convicts as settlers, the last about 1860. Australians are fiercely sensitive about this and assure you that rhyming slang is not used.

It is, however. (Australians spread it to California, where it is used today in California prisons.)

The rhyming slang depends on rhyme and humorous double meaning:

Storm-and-strife is the wife.

Bonnie fair is hair.

Gay-and-frisky is whisky. *Weeping willow* is a pillow.

"I went down to the little Jack Horner to buy a simple Simon for her lean-and-linger" equals "going down to the corner to buy a diamond for her finger."

The rhyming slang is especially sharp in the criminal field—*swinging door* is the word for prostitute. And *moan-and-wail* is jail.

As I say, I wouldn't throw it around. Let them use it. Taxi drivers are rich in it if you want to learn.

"Australians are very much like Americans. We both drive on the wrong side of the street; we both speak English with an hilarious accent; and we both have an outlandish money system."

—Interview with an Australian

You need a visa and an up-to-date smallpox vaccination certificate to land by ship or air at Sydney. Have it certified by your Board of Health. I came in a few years ago without such a certification. An Australian doctor gave me a needleful of something juicy—it took me a couple of days to recover.

The money is based on the English system—pounds, shillings, pence. All of which will be incomprehensible for a few days. You can start by learning that the two-shilling piece is a good tip for the bellboy.

Restaurant waiters are tipped 10 per cent. A quick way to figure this: Round off the bill into pounds. For example, 4 pounds, 10 shillings, and sixpence—5 pounds.

Two shillings is 10 per cent of a pound. Your tip then is 10 shillings.

About a shilling on the average taxi ride.

No health problems. You can drink the water anywhere. Good doctors and dentists available.

At the northern, tropical resorts, wear a hat against the sun.

Watch out for sunburn.

Wear rubber sneakers while skindiving or walking on the reefs. Coral cuts are bad. Coral breaks off in the cut and seems to go on growing. Swim from sandy beaches.

Bring in cigarettes (two cartons allowed). American cigarettes are subject to duty and are a little high. Plenty of English and Australian brands, which are good.

Liquor is not expensive. Scotch is the spirit drink. But Australians are mad about beer. It's very, very good and very, very strong. People from Sydney can't abide beer from Melbourne. And Melbourne people can't understand how they can drink that stuff they make in Sydney.

A real sleeper is the Australian table wine, which is excellent.

* * *

The continent is as large as the United States. It has only 10½ million people. Most of them live the urban life in Melbourne, Sydney, Brisbane, Perth, Canberra, and Adelaide.

The people are highly independent. If the hotel manager says you get early morning tea, drink it. He might come up and pour it down your throat.

Wages are not attractive enough to hold employees. And it is a constant problem for hotels to keep help. A Near East sheik on tour complained about the cooking in one of the big hotels. They asked him to leave.

"Because of your complaints, the chef just quit," they explained.

Australian food *was* pretty frightful.

Since the war, the country has opened the immigration gates. And the flood of Italians and Hungarians opened a number of very good restaurants.

As in every major metropolitan area, you have a large choice in this fast-growing city.

Native Australians, even more than Americans, think that food is somebody else's work. Therefore, the local cooking has been frightful. It inherited all the colonizing-English way of ruining food. It added to it the complete Australian independence.

Heaven knows you rarely meet an American cook or waiter who works at the job as a profession. They are all working temporarily while writing a book, it would seem.

The American Midwest is a desert amid plenty—a sort of reverse oasis.

If the fields are full of vegetables, the cook boils them to scalded death.

If the beef is the best corn-fed, he roasts it to a crisp. (This is also true of home cooking in the great American culinary desert that stretches between San Francisco and New York.)

The Australian cook simply didn't give a damn.

If you didn't like his cooking, go somewhere else. Where the food was just as bad.

Enter now the succulent years. The incoming Italians, French, and Hungarians opened their own restaurants. I think simply in self-defense. Before indigestion laid them low.

Sydney's King's Cross area is your best bet.

Sydney rock oysters surpass any other oysters in the world. If you are an oyster man, never start a meal without a dozen of these tasty things.

The longest oyster bar in the world is in Flinders Street in Melbourne.

Scene of the annual oyster-eating contest where Mr. Joe Barca downed 40 dozen in less than an hour.

"He had a loose throat, Joe Barca did," said the oyster man who was slitting them open for me.

The delightful custom is to eat these with brown bread and butter and a glass of Australian beer.

The restaurant protocol is a little peculiar, being geared to local liquor laws.

Until recently, the bars closed in Sydney at 6:30 during the height of what we would call the cocktail hour, and reopened at 7:30. That's changed now.

You can drink until 10 normally. Rules vary.

In Melbourne, all bars close at 6. This leads to the after-work 5-to-6 beer-drinking bust Australians call "the five-o'clock swill." Everybody gets as close to the bar as possible and downs beer as fast as he can. Worth getting into one of these some afternoon.

However, you can *order* your drinks when you book

for dinner early in the afternoon. Order more than you want. You don't have to take them or pay for them. As long as you order during drinking hours, you can be served after the hours. During dinner.

* * *

Swimming and yachting—Sydney Harbor is one of the world's greatest—are big sports.

The booming surf is full of sharks. The beaches have a lookout on shark patrol. He calls out the warning over a loudspeaker. The Australians take this shark patrol as a matter of course. But I never have nerve enough to get deeper than my waist. Wonderful surfing.

Racing is the spectator sport that drives Australians out of their blooming minds.

There are four race courses in metropolitan Sydney.

You have to see one of these—if nothing more than to see the bookmakers. Each under his own umbrella chalking up the changing odds with great skill and memory.

Bookmakers take bets only on first place.

If you want to bet place and show as well, you bet the track's windows. Odds based on the electrical totalizer.

I liked Warwick Farm track. Green and sunny and a pleasant way to spend the afternoon. (I never could get with the spaghetti sandwiches served at the stands. But maybe things have improved with the New Australians.)

Dress is country informal. Women will want cocktail dresses for evening. Men will need formal clothing only if they are going to a government function.

Downtown street wear in Sydney and Melbourne is like that in America.

Slacks and coats in the country. In the English fashion, ties and jackets are required in top restaurants.

Better not depend on buying clothing in Australia. Except for woolen sweaters, the price is not any better. And you probably won't like the cut.

Australians beeline off cruise ships in San Francisco and Los Angeles to buy off-the-rack American clothing.

Outside Sydney

Manly is a beach resort seven miles across the bridge. But it's more fun to go the half-hour by ferry. Good surf swimming and a promenade for viewing the pretty Australian girls.

The Blue Mountains are a couple of hours from Sydney. Usually included on a two-day tour offered by the travel agents.

I drove this one alone and was not too impressed. But maybe you should do it with a tour. Several tourist hotels—none that I saw looked great. Some falls, caves, and national parks.

If you have friends, a trip to a sheep station is well worth the time. In the outback everybody is connected by personal two-way radio. Kids even get their lessons by earphone. There's an impressive flying-doctor service.

You can hear some fascinating stories of the aborigines. Tame "abos" work on most of the stations but retain enough tribal background to give you a few shivers. Ask the people in the outback to tell you what happens when the tribal witch doctor "points the bone" at an enemy.

Melbourne

The conservative city. South and therefore colder. Take a topcoat. The farther south, the colder. And the seasons are reversed in Australia. Cold in July, steaming in December.

Collins Street is the pride of Melbourne. Lined with trees. Coffee houses and restaurants and the best hotels.

It's pleasant, quiet. The bars close at 6.

I bought a tie here (designed by a local artist) with

a tiny aborigine chasing a tiny kangaroo. During the war, they made our correspondent shoulder tabs at a local jeweler's. The Chevron Hotel dining room has good food.

Brisbane

Brisbane is the northern (and warmish) entrance to the Great Barrier Reef country. The coral reef runs 1200 miles along the Queensland coast.

It's for the people who want warm weather in the sun.

There are some fine boating trips to Hayman, Lindeman, and Green islands.

Many plans to build luxury hotels and develop all this country. And it will come along someday without doubt.

In Brisbane, the Majestic is now the best. Thirty-six renovated rooms.

The Carlton, the National, and the Gresham are fair hotels to base on.

Perth, Adelaide, and **Canberra** get very few tourists. These are for the leisurely exploration travelers.

Darwin in the primitive north is the center of the sheep country. **Alice Springs** for cattle.

Sydney Hotels

There are six hotels I'd consider here. I rate the Chevron-Hilton and the Carlton Rex a tie for the number-one choice. The Hotel Australia is a very close second. Followed by the Wentworth and the Hampton Court for third and fourth choices, and the Astra at Bondi Beach.

The Chevron-Hilton. Fairly new and modern. Too much chrome and glass for me, but many travelers prefer this type of hotel. It's in a good restaurant district, and there's a good view of Sydney harbor. They have a good dining room and a good floor show. And it's only five minutes by taxi to downtown.

The Carlton Rex. In the center of the city in Castlereagh Street off Martin Place. It's completely modernized. The Jet Bar is American style.

The Hampton Court. In King's Cross. Ten minutes from town by cab. Large rooms, good service. Part of Con Shaul's Federal Hotel chain.

The Australia. Also on Castlereagh Street. Once Sydney's leading hotel. The bar, just off the lobby, is still the best-known meeting place in town.

The Wentworth. An older well-known hotel in the downtown area. This is owned by Qantas Airways.

The Astra. At Bondi Beach, this one is a little out of town, but has a nice view and nice rooms. Long, white beach, with booming surf across the road.

Sydney Restaurants

Caprice. At Rose Bay. You must book in advance. It's only a few minutes' ride from downtown. With a view of Flying Boat Wharf. Try the Bombe Archduke dessert. Price is high. But worth it. This one is run by Jim Bendrodt and is a fine restaurant. Jim will try to tout you off the Australian wine—I think he feels you should drink French wine to give the place class. Don't let him. If you like wine, you'll be delighted with the Hunter River reds and whites.

The Elizabethan Room in the same area has an English air and English fare.

Prince's has a sort of Old-World elegance about it. The food is good and the clientele is upper level.

Romano's. 34 Castlereagh Street. Excellent food, good music, nice decor. (We used to come down to Romano's from New Guinea during the war.) Spend some time in the little piano bar before dinner. Very pleasant. I miss the old Oyster Bar here. It was a swinger.

Princess. 42 Martin Place. My choice for the French sauces. Try the mignonette à la Pierre, a split filet of beef. Prices here aren't so shocking.

Le Trianon. 29 Challis Avenue, in an old mansion. More French sauces. I like the coquilles St. Jacques. Outside terrace in summer.

Chelsea. 119 Macleay Road. Plenty plush. Perfume for the ladies on the house. But you'll find it sneaks into the check. Great service to go with the price.

Belvedere. 81 Baywater Road, King's Cross. I don't know this one. But they tell me it's pretty good. Continental. Different specialty every week. Not so plush.

Chalet. 3 Henrietta Lane. Madame Holdcregger serves up the Swiss-style fish.

Tulips. 250 George Street. Dutch-Javanese specialties.

Beppi's. St. James Flats at the corner of Yurong and Stanley streets. Italian menu. Satisfying. Small and not expensive.

Here are some others you might like:

The French Restaurant in Taylor Square, Darlinghurst. Don't worry, the entrance is the worst part. Would-be Left Bank.

Try the Coachman, 763 Bourke Street Redfern. A little pure English—gone Colonial. With costumes and all. The price is right.

The Adria at 8 King's Cross Road has truck-driver helpings.

The Buona Sera at 89 Macleay Street is Italian. What else?

Monseigneur at 61 Macleay offers flowers for the ladies. A Continental gesture to match the menu.

If you like veal, try Prunier at 440 New South Head Road.

Melbourne Hotels

Australia. Five dance floors in this partly air-conditioned hotel. Good arcade of shops.

Chevron-Hilton. Chrome and glass. What more can you say? This is no longer in Hilton's chain. But they keep the name.

Federal. Con Shaul's hotel here. At the quiet end of tree-lined Collins Street. Built in the Victorian Era.

Southern Cross. Big: 375 rooms and 43 suites. All air-conditioned. Music piped all over the place; 24-hour room service. You can get a shoeshine here in the barbershop. They're hard to find in Australia. Shoeshines, I mean. This is new. Has 80 shops, bowling, 4 restaurants, and 5 bars.

Menzies. Another Con Shaul Federal Hotel. Dancing every night. Also 24-hour room service.

Victoria. Has 565 rooms. But only 140 of them have private baths. No liquor license.

Melbourne Restaurants

There is a fair choice of restaurants in Melbourne. And espresso coffee shops. Many good Italian restaurants—which often serve Chinese food. Don't forget to try Australian wines. If you're not an expert, order Lindeman private bin. In reds and whites. There's a Rhinecastle private bin that's good too. But remember *private bin.*

The Ritz. Lonsdale Street. Luxury cuisine at luxury prices. Dimly lit atmosphere. Excellent service.

Antonio's. Toorak Road. In an old Victorian villa.

Maxim's. Fashionable for the young set.

Stromboli's. Toorak Road. Good choice of Australian wines here.

Maas Restaurant. High Street, St. Kilda. Cabaret atmosphere. Dancing and floor show on Saturdays.

George Hotel. St. Kilda. Dancing and floor show six nights a week. Smorgasbord.

Tarantella. Carlisle Street, St. Kilda. Ask for Mario. Good Italian food. With an informal, happy atmosphere. The waiters join in the entertainment. Open until 4:30 A.M.

Caprice. Top end of Collins Street. No liquor license, but the steaks couldn't be juicier. Wide selection of sandwiches.

Wentworth Café. Collins Street. For after the theater. English menu.

Ninky's. Top end of Collins Street in a mews; food in the Victorian manner.

Goldy's. Toorak Road, South Yarra. Another spot popular for the younger crowd. Lunch outside if you like.

For RUSSIAN atmosphere, cuisine, music, and dancing: **The Volga Volga** on Chapel Street in Prahran, or the **Troika** on the beach at Hampton.

Other ITALIAN restaurants you might like: The **Florentino** on Bourke Street and the **Society,** also on Bourke. (The Wine and Food Society meets here.) **Ricco's** on Spring Street or **Molina's** in the Imperial Hotel.

AUSTRIAN dishes can be had at **The Old Vienna Inn** on Russell Street.

The Ceylon Restaurant on Commercial Road for CURRY delights.

The City Kosher Café at 145 Russell Street should please the strictest Jewish tastes.

CHINESE FOOD should be pursued at **Lingman's,** Little Bourke Street. **China d'or** on Lonsdale. The **Chung Wah** on Heffernan Lane off Little Bourke Street. **Wing Hing and Wing Sun,** at the top of Bourke Street.

Jimmy Watson's on Carlton lets you pick your own steak for the barbecue.

Vegetarians can go to **The Naytura Café** on Little Collins Street.

The Gold Coast

Chevron. At Surfer's Paradise on Pacific Highway. Partly air-conditioned. Television. A hairdresser for the ladies. Dancing and floor shows. Swimming pool and squash court. A 24-lane indoor bowling center and deck tennis. Has 170 rooms, all with bath; a shopping arcade.

Lennons on the Gold Coast. At Broadbeach one mile south of Surfer's Paradise. Has 100 rooms, also with bath. Operated by Federal Hotels. Lots of activities. Free dancing lessons. Carnival nights, entertainment, beach picnics. Cost is about $135 for two weeks out of Sydney using a twin room with bath. All included.

Great Barrier Reef

Many islands you can visit. If you're on a tour, it's all arranged. On your own, the most popular seems to be Hayman Island.

Royal Hayman. In the Whitsunday Island group. On the southern part of the reef. The air-conditioned dining room looks over the swimming pool. (Floodlighted at night). Most European languages spoken. There are luaus and barbecues. Coral cruises and sightseeing. Catamaran and outrigger-canoe races. Reef, spear, and game fishing. Water skiing, skindiving, and bowls. Table and hard-court tennis. Oh, yes—and quoits. Or you can just laze under a shady tree in the tropical gardens.

Lindeman Island Resort is the best choice for conservative types.

Green Island and Heron Island are actually on the reef. **Barrier Reef House** on Green Island has new additions.

ELECTRICAL CURRENT

Voltage is 220–240, some AC, some DC. You'll need transformer plugs.

HOW TO GET THERE

Airlines: Air India, Ansett–ANA, BOAC, Canadian Pacific, KLM Royal Dutch, Pan American, Qantas, TEAL, Trans Australia, TAI.

Steamship Lines: Matson Navigation Company, P & O–Orient Lines, Royal Interocean Lines, and Shaw, Savill & Albion Co., Ltd.

CUSTOMS AND INOCULATIONS

All U.S. citizens will need a visa. British citizens, including Canadians of European descent do not. You'll need a smallpox shot. Also cholera and yellow fever if entering from other areas.

FOR MORE INFORMATION

Australian National Travel Association, 350 Post Street, San Francisco and 636 Fifth Avenue, New York City. Pacific Area Travel Association, 442 Post Street, San Francisco. And your carrier.

TO READ ALONG THE WAY

Great Barrier Reef and Adjacent Islands by Keith Gilbert and Frank McNeill; *Australia for the Visitor,* published by the Bank of New South Wales; *Land of the Southern Cross* by Bryce Kimear.

Tours

The outback is still desert and sheepland, and the tourist attractions are not particularly organized. (The interior only gets a couple of thousand tourists a year.) Actually, Australians themselves are the tourists—you find them all over the world marveling at things they could produce at home.

If there is one thing you will appreciate about Australia, it is that it *is* off the beaten path. You have to look for tours. And some of them are greatly rewarding.

The beaches are better than Waikiki. And you can have a whole Waikiki to yourself.

The desert lands are more exciting than Arizona. You can have them all to yourself.

If there are not all the glittering restaurants of Paris, there are some good ones. And you can get a table.

It's a country for discoveries. You have to work at it.

I think an Australian tour operator could make quite a bit of money. Get a fleet of Land Rovers, a few tame aborigines for color to hustle baggage. An Italian or Hungarian cook out of King's Cross in Sydney. And take off.

Great Barrier Reef Cruises ($70 for five days)
With so much empty country between cities, Australia has developed excellent airline service.

Fly north and base on Brisbane. Six hundred miles north of Brisbane, you catch cruise ships from Mackay and Proserpine. They are 24-passenger boats and sail every Tuesday. The five-day run stops at resort islands of Hayman, Lindeman, Brampton, and South Molle.

You swim on desert-island beaches and there's great deep-sea fishing.

Go to Cairns, a thousand miles north of Brisbane (and remember going north you are getting into warm, tropical country) and you can make day trips to the Reef each day.

Launch service operates at 9:30 A.M. to Green Island, a land of palm trees perched right on top of the famous reef. Time to get there is only an hour.

They show you the Reef itself through glass walls of an underwater observatory. You can hire a glass-bottom boat. Or you can actually walk on the Reef at low tide.

The water is crystal-clear and the coral formations are fantastic.

This island is being developed for the tourist. You can stay overnight or longer in the new lodges. It's cheap enough. The boat costs $1.50 round trip and room and meals are $7 a day.

The tourist air fare from Brisbane to Cairns and back to Brisbane is $78.

This is tropical north Australia. For $9.50 you can take the day tour to the Atherton Tableland—rainforests, waterfalls, lakes, tropical flowers, and a return to Cairns along the Gillies Highway, which skirts a magnificent coastline for miles and miles.

Gold Coast Tours ($6.25 for one day out of Brisbane)
This is Australia's Miami and well built up for tourist trade. Long beaches of white sand with a surf that rolls for a thousand blue miles.

Hundreds of motor inns, hotels, apartments for rent, and guest houses.

Well-known resorts are Surfer's Paradise, Coolangatta, and Tweed Heads.

Friday and Sunday are the motor-coach day tours for $6.25. But you can go any day by private car at a cost of $7.50 each for four.

Outback Tour ($41 for one day)
This is a flying trip from Sydney into the sheep-station country. You leave early (weekdays only) and fly to Bathhurst or Dubbo, where you are met by a driver-guide.

The day tour takes you to sheep stations and farms. You see wild kangaroos and wild birdlife.

Sydney Tour (You do it on your own for about $3)
Take a taxi in the morning down to Circular Quay and catch the Manly Ferry across the harbor to Manly on the narrow isthmus between Sydney's lovely harbor and the booming Pacific. Sailing time is 35 minutes.

There's a fine surf beach with pine trees. Surf carnivals in the summer—there's a big thing in Australia of life-saving teams. Lunch at Manly and take a taxi ($1.50) over Spit Bridge to Taronga Park Zoo.

This is an excellent zoo. It's on a hillside, so don't walk up (as I did). There's a bus. Take the bus to the top and stroll down through the zoo.

You get all of isolated Australia's strange animals here. Everything seems to develop in a pouch in this

odd land. A nice, tree-shaded zoo and a pretty view of the harbor.

At the bottom of the hill, there's a pleasant ferry service to downtown Sydney.

Blue Mountain Tour ($18.50 for two days)

I drove this in my own rented car, and maybe that was a mistake. Or maybe the Blue Mountains simply don't come up to the Rockies or the Tyrol.

I didn't think too much of it scenically or for fun. But maybe the $18.50 guided tour by bus would be better.

These leave Sydney each Wednesday and Saturday.

You go west 115 miles through suburbs, small towns, bushland, and the Blue Mountains. A feature of the trip is Jenolan Caves. You stay overnight at Caves House and see the limestone caves. These were once coral mountains under the ocean. The area is a government wild-life preserve.

Sydney–Canberra–Melbourne Tour ($37.50 for three days)

These leave Sydney every Saturday and Monday morn-

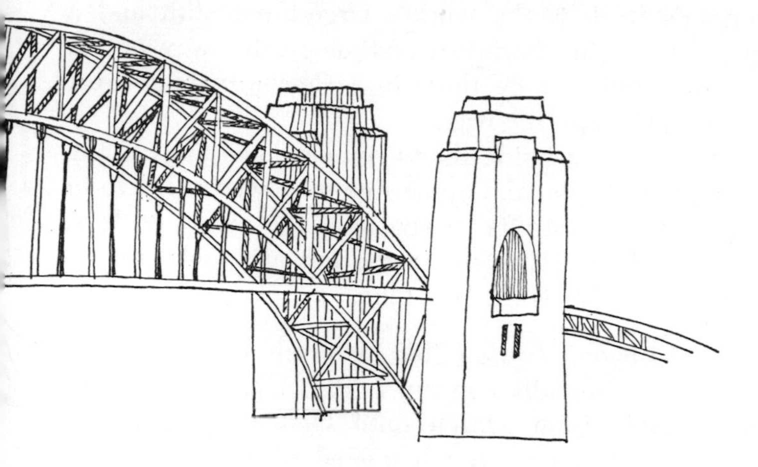

ing. Spend the first night out near Canberra, the national capital. Next day visit Canberra's sights—Parliament House, the Australian War Memorial Museum, the National University. It's a pretty city with attractive gardens.

On the way to Gundagai for the second night, you go through sheep farms and bushland.

The next day is en route Melbourne. Mainly fruit-growing areas.

Melbourne is a pleasant town. The scene of *On the Beach* with Ava Gardner, in which the whole world dies of nuclear poisoning. If you gotta go, you might as well go in Melbourne.

Catch the longest oyster bar in the world. It's in Flinders Street. The rock oysters are opened right at the bar. The Melbourne beer is good and will knock your hat off.

Ayer's Rock Tour ($53 from Alice Springs)
Alice Springs is *the* town in the middle of the country. Serves the outback with movies, shopping, and a night in town.

Ayer's Rock is the world's largest monolith and a sacred thing in aboriginal mythology. It's way out in nowhere and you fly there in a Cessna, passing over cattle stations on the way.

At the rock, a guide shows you cave paintings of the aboriginal people—the Stone-Age men who still live in the north of Australia. If you have the wind and legs, you can climb 1100 feet to the top and look around. April to October is the best time.

Back of Beyond Tours ($166 for seven days)
These tours actually can run 7, 10, 13, or 22 days. Out of Adelaide from March until October (the cooler months). They go through rugged cattle country like the American Old West. Through opal fields, desert areas, and the outback of Central Australia.

Transportation is by Land Rover. This is the British jeep—a four-wheel drive and a rugged car. You camp at night. See real wild aborigines, mobs of kangaroos, wild birds, wild dogs. A trip for the adventurous.

Barossa Valley Tour ($3.50 for the day)
This is a short trip out of Adelaide to the wine country. And the wines are excellent.

You go on this one by rail to Nuriootpa and tour the grape valley.

Lunch at Vine Inn and see the Seppeltsfield winery.

Tasmania Tour ($27.85 for two days)
This rather quaint island outpost has small fishing villages and old architecture. There's a two-day, share-car tour year round between the towns of Hobart and Launceston.

Overnight stop in picturesque St. Helen's overlooking the South Tasman Sea. Plenty of sightseeing along the coast and a sort of view of Australia as it used to be.

Port Arthur Tour (***Tasmania***) ($4.50 for one day)
The last of England's exported convicts were sent to Tasmania in about 1860. Port Arthur is where they landed, and there are stone walls and other memories of those days. It's now a place of wild roses on the beautiful Tasman Peninsula.

A one-day tour out of Hobart via Eaglehawk Neck. Good coastal scenery.

ONE MORE THING. I have a friend, name of Fred Holmes, who's crazy about sheep ranches. Just loves them . . . and says if you miss a visit to one, you miss Australia. I don't know. I never made a sheep ranch. I leave that to you. And Fred Holmes. Same-day-return air flights to selected sheep stations.

NEW ZEALAND

Still is the steam cloud shining fair,
'Tis a white pall, hanging ever there,
O'er a tomb that none can see.
But the draping fern fronds are no more glad;
Karapiti's moan is a* tangi *sad
And a warning voice to the Maori lad
Who false to his tryst would be.

Few consider what a savage man is, in his natural state, and even after he is in some degree civilized. The New Zealanders are certainly in some state of civilization; their behaviour to us was manly and mild, showing on all occasions a readiness to oblige. They have some arts among them which they execute with great judgment and unwearied patience; they are far less addicted to thieving than the other islanders of the South Sea; and I believe those in the same tribe, or such as are at peace one with another, are strictly honest among themselves. This custom of eating their enemies slain in battle (for I firmly believe they eat the flesh of no others) has, undoubtedly, been handed down to them from the earliest times; and we know it is not an easy matter to wean a nation from their ancient customs, let them . . . be ever so inhuman and savage; especially if that nation has no manner of connection or commerce with strangers. For it is by this that the greatest part of the human race has been civilized; an advantage which the New Zealanders from their situation never had. An intercourse with foreigners would reform their manners, and polish their savage minds. Or, were they more united under a settled form of government, they would have fewer enemies; consequently, this custom would be less in use, and might in time be in a manner forgotten.

—*from Cook's* Journal, *second voyage; November 1773*

MONEY. New Zealand pounds ($2.80 U.S. to 1 pound)

BEST TIME TO GO. Local spring and fall.

LANGUAGE. English with a strong touch of "Home," as England is known to these faraway people. Many of them have never been "Home." But they honor the Queen and the traditions, eat Christmas pudding in the heat of December 25 summer, and put up with frightful English cooking of half a century ago.

The English of New Zealand has less twang than does that of neighboring Australia.

The Australian says *bloody* (offensive in England). The New Zealander says something I find unprintable. Also offensive in England. Nonetheless, New Zealand whites don't mind referring to themselves as *pakehas.*

The so-and-so word comes out in the Maori name for white man—*pakeha,* which is supposed to be a phonetic corruption of the much-used word.

A number of Maori words have gone into the language in place and object names.

There is no rhyming slang, as in Australia. And American slang words don't seem to have stretched Down Under into the teen-age groups as they have to more accessible parts of the world.

Apparently the distance keeps New Zealand's English pure.

As you leave the airport at Sydney, Australia, there is a free-port shop where you can order American cigarettes, liquor, transistor radios, perfume. All highly desirable and expensive in New Zealand.

The New Zealand Airline TEAL flies you across. In spite of an energetic tourist office, there aren't many tourists to New Zealand. And not much to do.

The restaurant and night spot recommended to me

is the Hi Diddle Griddle—a rather drafty place. And rather expensive (for fried chicken), since they were paying for the services of a piano player and bass-fiddle plucker.

Bars close at 6 P.M., throwing out into the chilly Auckland streets a covey of cocktail fans. Too late to drink, too early to go home.

For the tourist, the hotel bar is open. (Under the old English rule that a man is entitled to food and drink and oats for his horse at all hours.)

New Zealand is much more oriented to Home—England—than Australia is.

New Zealanders are proud of being volunteer settlers from Home. (Australia's first settlers were convicts, sent out because England could no longer send them to America. We were loaded until the Revolution.)

Not as outwardly independent, and more law-abiding than the don't-give-a-damn Aussies. Yet I must say that there is some mild bootlegging in the touristy restaurants. (They slip it to you under the table.)

I was unable to find the late "sly grog shop" so beloved by the Australian.

Nor the illegal "two-up" gambling games, as I could in Sydney.

* * *

The major attraction is the sporting life. You can catch swordfish and mako shark at sea. A number of varieties of trout (rainbow trout were imported from California). In New Zealand waters they grow to incredible size.

Deer, originally imported from England, have no natural enemies here. Consequently, they have grown so thick that the government hires game wardens to thin them out by shooting.

You get salmon and brown trout in the South Island. Rainbow in North Island—where Auckland is located.

Like Australia, it gets colder as you go south.

Seasons are the reverse of ours—winter is warm, summer is cold.

New Zealanders have the English habit of keeping their hotels chill. I came directly from the tropics in September, the New Zealand spring. All the hotels had their doors open to the 55-degree weather.

Everybody sat around in overcoats, apparently enjoying it immensely.

Take a sweater—two sweaters. And an overcoat.

* * *

The original Polynesian Maoris stand equally with the white New Zealander. No color bar. The Maoris are 7 per cent of a 2½-million population.

They migrated in the great canoe migrations about 1350. Coming on a land short of meat animals, they polished off the ancient moa—an ostrich-size bird.

Then they started eating each other.

The present-day food leaves a lot to be desired. I nearly polished off the bellboy myself.

The hotel food I found impossible. I wouldn't say it was gourmet country.

It's sheep country. Truly beautiful on a sunny day to see thousands of white sheep on the green hills.

There is good boating and good surf swimming in the Tasman Sea. Good beaches a few miles from Auckland.

You can drink the water anywhere. Tipping is milder than at home. Tip only for special services.

Taxis are cheap enough. Prices are not high in hotels. But, I think, high for what you get. Rooms are rather small. Hotels usually crowded.

Auckland is a pretty town, swept by sea breezes. The white wooden houses give it some of the look of Cape Cod or Monterey, California.

The people are very friendly. Not so reserved as the English.

Seafood is good. There is a clam here called Toheroa that makes a delicious soup.

You drive on the left, as in Australia. Tea is the big drink—morning and afternoon. You need a visa on your passport. Customs is pretty thorough. They don't get too many people coming in. Electric current is 230 volts, 50 cycles. Both AC and DC.

If you want unspoiled country—the way it was—New Zealand is your land.

Auckland Hotels

De Brett: Considered Auckland's best.

Great Northern: The big one: 147 rooms, 31 with baths. Just average. With average prices (About $10.50 single).

The Station Hotel: The Pacific Area Travel Association likes this one. Small. Harbor view for diners.

About 12 other hotels in Auckland. None of them seems to be up to the standards set elsewhere in the Pacific. Perhaps the traffic until now hasn't warranted a plush job. There will probably be some building-up there soon.

Christchurch Hotels

The hotel situation isn't the greatest here, either. There is the United Service Hotel. Downtown. Golf a half-mile away.
Or Warners Hotel. Or the White Hart.

Resort Hotels—North Island

Waitomo Hotel: Near the Waitomo Caves and the famous Glowworm Grotto.

Wairakei Hotel: Lots of geysers. Mineral baths. Also golf, tennis, trout fishing.

Waikaremoana Lake House: More fishing, hiking, boating.

Takaanu Hotel: At Lake Taupo. Fish.

Chateau Tongariro: In Tongariro National Park. All-year mountain resort. Golf, hiking. Winter sports in season.

Resort Hotels—South Island

Milford Hotel: Milford Sound, New Zealand's fiordland. Cruises and excursions.

Eichardt's Hotel: Skiing in winter, boat trips in summer. On Lake Wakatipu.

Te Anau Hotel: Some of New Zealand's spectacular scenery on display at Lake Te Anau. As you would expect, fishing.

Auckland Restaurants

Gourmet: Run by a Dutchman. Standard Continental.

Hi Diddle Griddle: It's there, all right. Tell them to close the window.

Tours

Pan American flies directly into Auckland from Honolulu via Samoa. Or you fly across from Australia on the New Zealand TEAL airline.

The country is far-side-of-the-world British Colonial. It has a feeling of still being built. A little of the rugged self-discipline of the American Midwest a hundred years ago.

It is scenic country. Sportsman's country. Deer are so thick that the government hires men to thin them out by shooting. And rainbow trout, descendants of California's imports, grow to great size.

There are two major islands—North and South.

The total is about like California. There are good beaches and some skiing.

Tours are arranged by the New Zealand Government Tourist Bureau. They are made for independent (not group) travel. You can ask for variations. They are reversible—that is, you can start or depart from Auckland, Wellington, or Christchurch.

They don't operate on set dates. You can start any day.

You can go by scheduled air, bus, or train. Or you can go by private car.

It's a nice, loose arrangement for people who want a leisurely trip without regimentation.

Tour Na–50 ($136.50 for six days)
Arrive at Auckland the first day. (You can arrange a sightseeing tour of the city if you like. The white farm houses have a New England look and Auckland's setting from the air is pretty.)

Second day takes you from Auckland to Waitomo Caves, including the Glowworm Grotto. The road goes through green pastureland. (If you start counting sheep in New Zealand, you'll never make it.) Four hours for this part.

Third day takes you from the caves to Rotorua—four hours. There's a model Maori village here that's inter-

esting. Showing how the native Polynesian lived between times of raiding the neighbors. The carved Maori church at Ohinemutu I found interesting.

Fourth day you stay at Rotorua. Some Maori souvenir shops, but mostly carved replicas of the wooden figures you see at the model village.

Fifth day takes you back through farming and sheep country to Auckland. Five hours.

There is a seven-day tour covering about the same ground with an additional day at Wairakei. This valley of steaming craters has been harnessed to provide electrical power and the steam escapes rather prosaically in safety-valve bursts from powerhouse pipes.

However, there are trips to places where the steam bubbles naturally. And the hotel is very pleasant. The seven-day tour is number Na–58.

Tour Na–51 ($231 for 11 days)
Approximately the same as Na–50 with addition of Chateau Tongariro, Wanganui, and Wellington, the capital. Returns via New Plymouth. Chateau Tongariro is a mountain resort.

Tour Na–52 ($364 for 12 days)
This takes you to both North and South islands. The North Island portion is through the Waitomo, Rotorua,

Wairakei regions. You then fly to South Island (five hours) to Dunedin.

The last five days of the trip are over Milford Sound. To Queenstown and up to Mount Cook and some sightseeing in Christchurch.

There are also 15- and 16-day tours.

The top tour is 41 days ($868) that covers just about everything.

* * *

If I were doing this myself, I'd have the tourist office set up a hand-tailored tour that covered some back-country fishing. Except for the geysers, the fiords, and the glacier ride, the countryside is much the same to look at.

AND ANOTHER THING

Since sightseeing is the major attraction, visitors are usually taken on a full day's drive to Rotorua (where there is a Maori village restored) and Wairakei, the steamy producer of electric power.

The underground steam has been harnessed by "bores" —a few vagrant puffs float into the air. There is a pleasant hotel alongside. If you have plenty of imagination, you can think how it was in Maori days. Very steamy.

On the hotel wall is a florid poem commemorating a Maori girl who leaped into one of these boilers when her boy friend stood her up.

* * *

Waitomo has a series of caves where stalactite meets stalagmite. Glowworm Grotto is a scary sort of place where you ride an underground river into a grotto lighted by obliging glowworms. If you make a noise, they shut off the built-in electricity.

* * *

South Island's main features are offshore fishing and ski-planing up to the glaciers.

You fly up in four-seat Astras from the resort hotel, the Hermitage.

They land you right on the glacier. For expert skiers, there's a 16-mile run down the ice.

Spectacular scenery—and if you like to count sheep, South Island has got millions of them. Hotels in Christchurch are not elegant. But fishing and hunting on South Island are supposed to be the greatest.

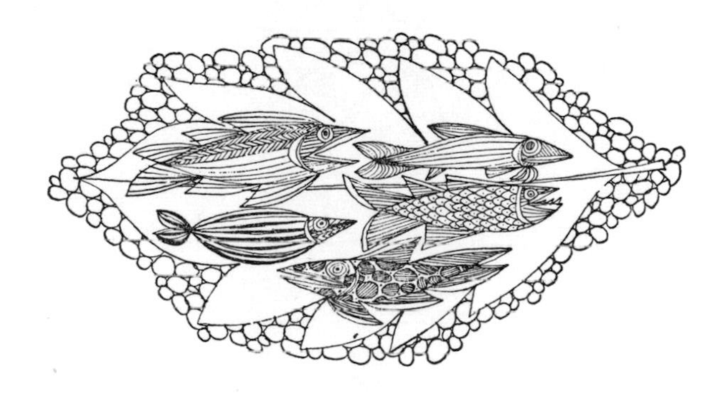

TAHITI

"I think this* tiki *no more live.
I think this* tiki *dead."

I got up to take leave, when the women, in a very obliging manner, came to me with a mat, and a piece of their finest cloth, which they put on me after the Otaheite fashion. When I was thus dressed, they each of them took one of my hands, and accompanied me to the waterside, and at parting promised that they would soon return my visit.

—Captain William Bligh, voyage to Otaheite, 1787

MONEY. 80–90 Pacific francs to $1 U.S.

BEST TIME TO GO. May through September. The most popular time is July 13–20 for the Bastille Day celebrations.

LANGUAGE. French and Tahitian.

French Polynesia—Tahiti, the Tuamotus, the Gambiers, the Îles-sous-les-Vent—speak Tahitian at home and French in the schools.

Samoa, the Cook Islands, New Zealand Maoris, and independent Tonga Islands use English.

The hula—standing or sitting—is a communication of legend with a dominant theme in all the islands. This is the hula that tells of the great canoe migrations: the farewell songs to the native land, the long voyage, the

despair and tiring at the paddles, the triumphant discovery of the new land.

It's a pleasant little fiction that Tahiti is now "spoiled" by tourists.

When I was first here in 1956, the happy island had 67 visitors in the entire year.

In 1963, thanks to the new jet strip and airline flights, the tourist office counted 50,000.

The difference now is you can get a good tropical hotel room instead of the broken-down four-poster I had before. And you can get a very good French-cooked dinner instead of eating inferior pork-fried noodles at an oilcloth-covered table in a Chinese short-order house.

* * *

There are some impressive maps showing enormous hotel developments. But they will be a long time building.

The native Tahitian doesn't like to build hotels.

He likes to fish a little. Pick a breadfruit off the tree in the back yard. Make love a little. And sleep a lot.

The French won't bring in outside labor. (Hawaii was built and run by industrious Chinese and Japanese.) The Tahitian's wants are simple: a couple of bottles of the local Hinano beer on Saturday night.

He is not tempted by radios, outdoor barbecues, or television sets.

In this lovely climate, a wraparound *pareu* or a pair of shorts is clothing enough.

The Tahitian decorates himself with a crown of fresh flowers he weaves himself while riding on *le truck*—the open-air bus that goes around the island.

The get-up-and-go hotel builders go out of their minds trying to get enough pandanus thatch—a local product throughout the 110 islands of the Society group.

Pandanus is woven when the mood is on.

From the hilltops, Bounty Bay sparkles with blue-diamond water exactly as it did for the ferocious Captain Bligh.

Point Venus is a tropical grove of black sand and coco palm parabolas. Just as it was when Captain James Cook observed the transit of Venus in 1769.

The waterfall described in *The Marriage of Loti* tumbles into a lush haven of green. Tahitian girls still drop their bright print *pareus* to bathe in the silky waters falling from the cloud-topped peaks.

It's the island of dreams.

* * *

You need a French visa and a return ticket to get through the gates at Faaa Airport. (If you have an onward ticket, you can stop over for short stays without the visa.)

The new jet strip is built out on the coral reef—there isn't enough flat land on the island. We used to come in by slow Solent flying boat, two days of flying from Suva in the Fijis.

French Customs are thorough. If you bring in a camera, you must take it out again. No question but that dollar tourists are bumping prices up and taking over some of the local girls.

The French Colonials are not happy about it. I don't blame them.

But *c'est la vie Tahitienne*. You enter without problems.

Better bring in cigarettes. You are allowed 1 carton. The local price for American cigarettes is 35 cents or more a pack.

Tipping is *tapu*—a word you should learn. The entrance marked *tapu* means "don't enter."

Don't tip the boy who carries your bag. Don't tip the taxi driver. Don't tip the waitress. If you feel you have to do something, go down to the Chinese stores in Papeete. Buy her a *pareu*-length of the loudest print you can find.

The Tahitian girl competes with an island full of flaming hibiscus.

When you see the morning traffic of putt-putt bicycles, the print *pareus,* and the long black hair streaming down girls' backs, it's like watching a parade of tropical flowers.

French is the official language. Tahitian is the home language. Your room girls learned French like you did. In school. They speak it more slowly and your high school French works in a way to make your teacher proud of you.

No health problems. You can drink the water and eat anything.

Mosquitoes may bite you in the hill country. But the breeze blows them away down at the beach. Anyway, there's a Flit spray gun under your bed.

* * *

Papeete is a sandy banana-palm town of 20,000. A dollar taxi ride from your hotel.

It's what a tropical town should look like: seagoing, salt-stained yachts along the waterfront. A little gray French gunboat with sailors in white shorts, and red pompon caps. Open-front Chinese stores with hardware hanging from the rafters and bright print cloth spilling on the counters.

The little chug-chug boat for the island of Moorea loading pigs and chickens and flower-wreathed, brown Tahitians.

Cargo schooners putting up sail for the piled copra

waiting beside sandy lagoons in the atolls of the Tuamotus.

One walk around town and you've seen the sights. (However, they have values on repetition.)

Better change some money to Pacific francs.

They're hard to get back into dollars because of currency control. Don't cash more than you intend to spend.

Chez Chapiteau is the place for lunch. About the same food you would get in a good, medium Paris restaurant. But served by a barefoot brown girl with black hair hanging to her waist.

French wine is cheap. Local custom is to put a chunk of ice in it. Whether it's red or white. Most of it comes from Algeria.

Scotch and bourbon are expensive. But the French bring in a nice light rum from Martinique, their island in the Caribbean. You can get an icy punch of rum, sugar, and the flavorful island lime.

The grapefruit here are the size of cannonballs. And breadfruit is better than you think.

You can rent scooters at a reasonable price. Car rentals are high. About $50 a week for a small French Simca or Renault.

You must drive around the island once. It takes the comfortable part of a day. Stop at Faratea, halfway around. Excellent food.

Laundry is fast and not expensive.

You can wear almost anything you like. I wear khaki pants, an aloha shirt, and sandals.

Drugstores are not the gadget departments we have at home. But they have all the modern medicines you might need. French doctors and dentists for emergencies.

* * *

Papeete comes alive at night. What the "night clubs" lack in decor, they make up for in enthusiasm.

Le tweest gets all mixed up here with the hip-vibrating Tahitian hula.

I'd certainly take in Quinn's Tahitian Hut. Stay on Hinano beer—the cloudy Pernod favored by the girls in Quinn's is made for other stomachs than yours or mine.

Bar Lea is a lively, crowded dancing place. Been getting a little rough lately.

At midnight, everybody goes a couple of miles out of town to Lafayette, a coco-log, pandanus-thatch place where the dancing really goes wild.

For the more decorous, there's very good music at Spence Weaver's beautiful Hotel Tahiti.

Tip: Take off your shoes and dance barefoot with the waitress. It's more fun.

* * *

Tahiti doesn't offer much tourist shopping. (Tahitians can't be bothered carving native handicrafts for the tourist trade. Any more than you can get them to build hotels.)

The shell necklaces are good and inexpensive.

A couple of industrious French are making heavy linen aloha shirts or skirts with hand-blocked Tahitian prints.

Marie Ah You on the waterfront street Quai Bir Hackeim will run you up a dress for about $10. (If you have business in Tahiti, Father Ah You is the Big Business.)

You can buy carved wooden drums and carved wooden *tikis.* But you have to ship them. Too heavy.

Don't buy stone *tikis.*

A stone *tiki* is a living god and he doesn't like to be moved.

Spence Weaver moved a stone *tiki* onto the lawn at Hotel Tahiti. He just about lost all his help—it was that bad luck.

Jimmy, the taxi driver, is a *tahuna,* a priest.

He finally determined the stone *tiki* had died. "I think this *tiki* no more live. I think this *tiki* dead," Jimmy told me.

He was plenty relieved. "If he live *tiki,* he walk at night. Unless you chain him."

* * *

You can buy some hula skirts made of off-white fiber. (They also make a shell-and-fiber bra—for girls going formal.)

And that's about it.

Except—every night buy a *tiare Tahiti* to tuck behind your ear—the fragrant little jasmine flower of the island.

It's the custom for both men and women. And a better signal than a wedding ring.

Behind the right ear, you are taken.

Behind the left ear—"*On cherche,*" said the Tahitian girl who told me about this pleasant custom.

There's good fishing off the island and the water is a painter's blue. You can rent or charter anything from an outrigger to a schooner.

Skindiving is great. A wonderful variety of rainbow fish around the reef and some fine shells. You can rent all the equipment through your hotel.

For tours and information, there's Poroi Tours. (The boss is mayor of Papeete.)

They work out that overnight trip to the island of Moorea. That peaked island you look at each evening. With a golden glow of sunset behind the dark hills and a big, frosted rum punch in your hand. The Bali H'ai of *South Pacific.*

If you run into Eddie Lund, you'll discover a knowledgeable American who's been recording music here for many years.

Ralph Varady is always around. Usually manager of

Hotel Tahiti. He knows the outer islands better than anyone.

Take a look at Jean Masson's paintings if he's at home. It's a wading, barefoot walk to his house out at Point Venus. But he's a fine painter.

Vaima on the waterfront is the morning-and-afternoon coffee house.

Watch the people and the passing parade.

There aren't any lost Gauguins floating around. But you might—just might—run into a Leeteg painting on black velvet. They're getting valuable. Poor Leeteg got full of rum one night and ran his scooter into a concrete bridge.

The Outer Islands

RAI flying boats go to some of the Tuamotus. These are the low-lying atolls—coral-formed as compared with the "high islands," which are volcanic.

There are no hotels. You can sleep in some family's pandanus hut.

Strictly for the adventurous.

There's pearl-shell diving. And on one island, the boys ride sharks just for the hell of it.

This is an expanding service, however. May be better as time goes along.

Ralph Varady in Papeete is a good source on these islands. Good many wrecks, famous ones. They call the chain "The Dangerous Archipelago."

Bora Bora is served by RAI DC-4s. They land on an old American bomber strip.

This *is* the most beautiful island in the world. It's a shame to write about it. A high island, wreathed in clouds. A turquoise lagoon. White-sand beaches—but

in *all* these islands, don't wade. Keep your feet off the bottom. They've got a spiny stone fish. Step on him and you are sick.

An excellent, modern hotel, the Bora Bora.

Good food. Good accommodations. The skindiving equipment is on the house.

There's a town of Vaitape. One tiny hotel. Two Chinese stores. It costs a $6 taxi ride to get there from the hotel and most people pass it up.

But for a lovely island, the way a South Sea island should be, Bora Bora is it.

Tahiti Hotels

Tahiti. The action spot on the happy isle. Ask for Ralph Varady. Or Spence Weaver, who owns the hotel. Varady knows more about the South Seas than most people you'll meet. Food is good, and the dancing in the evening is lively. The swimming pool should be ready now.

Or you can skindive from the pier. Once a week there's a Tahitian dance group in for the show.

Rates: $12, $14, $17 single, $15, $17, $20 double. For full American plan, add $11.50 per person. For modified American plan, add $8.

Taaone. Another plush spot, a little quieter than the Tahiti. Exceptional food, and an attractive black-sand beach. About two miles from town. Dancing every night, and a Tahitian show once a week.

Rates: $15.50 single, $18 double.

Tahiti Village. Ten miles west of Papeete. Rent a car if you stay here. It is big and another very plush operation. Food is fair, there's dancing (occasionally), and the white-sand beach is one of the best on Tahiti. Water skiing and tennis court.

Rates: $15 to $18.

Tiki Tapu. Pleasant cottages, fair food. Hiro Levy is the owner, but he is hardly ever there. The *tapu tiki* is in the drive, close to the reception area. Look but don't touch—unless you're not superstitious. It's a stone *tiki.* They're bad news in this part of the world.

Rates: $7 to $14, single or double.

Matavai. Next door to the Tiki Tapu. One mile from town, at the entrance to the Tipaerui Valley. They tell me there is a swimming pool, but I never saw one there. Again the price is right for Tahiti: $9 to $14 for bungalows, $11.25 for one of the 10 attached units.

Arihiri. Two and a half miles from Papeete. Outriggers available for guests.

Bel Air. They don't like to accept single men here. Four and a half miles from town with a swimming pool. Pirogues, and a catamaran free to guests.

Lotus Village. Six miles from Papeete. Tahitian-style bungalows, snack bar.

Iaorana Villa. Seven miles from town, has a good beach front. Outriggers available.

Princess Heiata. Near the Taaone in the Pirae district. Black-sand beach.

Faratea. Halfway round the island, at the point joining Tahiti-iti. Great food in the French manner. Stop on your island tour and have them tell you about their trip to the small *motu* here. Great for an overnight stay. Or just for the afternoon.

Restaurants

Let's face it. The food here isn't the greatest. The best I've found is at:

Chez Chapiteau. Right in town. Sit on the balcony and watch the native girls buzz by on their Vespas. M. Chapiteau made his reputation at the old Les Tropiques. He's good.

Hotel Tahiti. Best food on the island.

Hotel Taaone. Beautiful French table service, fine food. Get the open wine.

Waikiki. Chinese food. Eat it at your own risk.

Night Clubs and Entertainment

Vaima. For the best entertainment: people-watching. During the day. Go early in the morning, dip your French bread in the thick black coffee and see them load the ships for Moorea. This is near the market and next door to Quinn's. The action is amazing.

Quinn's. Right out of the days of Bully Hayes and the sailing ships. Wild. French sailors in red pompon hats. Waterfront girls dancing *le tweest,* and tourists looking shocked at the coeducational John.

Bar Lea. Plenty Tahitian, a little rough for most tourists. Action about the same as Quinn's. Go after 10 P.M. for the rock 'n roll.

Lafayette. Wildest dancing in the Pacific. Everybody goes about midnight and dances till the band wears out. This opens when the other places close. You've got to see this one. Once.

Hotel Tahiti. Best orchestra for dancing. Most dressy place on the island.

Shopping

All along the Quai Bir Hackeim for shellwork, pearls, woven hats, grass skirts, *tikis,* other souvenir stuff. Careful, a lot of this stuff doesn't look so good when you get it home.

Marie Ah You makes great dresses from original wood-block-printed *pareu* cloth. **Tiki** has good souvenirs. Sylvain for photo supplies. Dave Cave–Hertz; Max Provost–Avis. Gustave Martin on the Rue Jeanne d'Arc –jewelry, watch repair. René Pailloux–mother-of-pearl, grass skirts, souvenirs.

Sightseeing and Tours

City Tour. Pamatai Heights, Queen Marau's burial place, Governor's Mansion, Qui Bir Hackeim, Pirae for a swim from the black-sand beach, and lunch at the Hotel Taaone.

Circle Island. Completely around the main part of the island. King Pomare's Benedictine-bottle grave, Heights of Taharaa (One Tree Hill), Point Venus, Captain Cook's landing place, Blowhole of Arahoho. Lunch at Faratea, then to an ancient Tahitian place of worship, Marae Arahurahu.

Moorea. The Bali H'ai island can be visited for 24 hours, two days, or longer. You must do this just to see Pau Pau Bay, one of the most beautiful in the world.

Bora Bora. One hour by RAI. I like this so much I don't know whether to recommend it or not. I'd like to keep it secret. The most beautiful island in the world, without question. The food is French at the Hotel Bora Bora, the girls are pretty, and the skindiving equipment is on the house. The colors in the lagoon are too beautiful to describe. Go and see for yourself.

HOW TO GET THERE

Airlines: Pan American Airlines, TEAL (Tasman Empire Airways Ltd.), TAI (Transports Aériens Intercontinentaux).

Steamship Lines: Matson Navigation Company, New Zealand Shipping Co., Ltd., Shaw Savill & Albion Co., Ltd., Union Steam Ship Co. of New Zealand.

VISAS AND CUSTOMS

You need a visa from the French consul if you stay more than 72 hours. Smallpox vaccination is all that is required.

WHEN TO GO

Almost all year around. May to November are probably best. The heaviest rain (and I mean *heavy!*) falls between December and March. Temperature averages about 77 all year.

ELECTRICAL CURRENT

110 AC–U.S. type.

TO READ ON THE WAY

The Marriage of Loti, White Shadows of the South Seas, Many Lagoons, written by Ralph Varady; Barnaby Conrad's *Tahiti; People of Many Islands* by Bill Brown; and *Adventures in Paradise* by Willard Price.

FOR MORE INFORMATION

Your carrier will have useful information, and you can get further notes from The Syndicate Initiatif, Quai Bir Hackeim, and Pacific Area Travel Association, 442 Post Street, San Francisco.

Samoa

TEAL, the New Zealand airline, flies Electras in a one-day flight from Tahiti to Fiji via American Samoa.

There is a light-plane service from American Samoa to Western Samoa, a lovely set of islands with Apia as the main town.

There are two hotels, both a little primitive.

I'd stay at Aggie Grey's on the waterfront. Scottish beer on the back porch. Pigs in the yardful of hibiscus and flame trees everywhere.

The Samoans are the architects of the South Seas. Their villages are beautiful circles of open-air, thatched houses. If it rains or blows, they let down a sort of Venetian blind of coco matting on that side.

The grass is scythed down every day. And each village sits in a grove of curving coco palms.

The wraparound *lava lava* is the native dress. I wear one myself at Aggie Grey's.

Not as gay as Papeete—though Apia in the days of Bully Hayes was known as "The Hellhole of the Pacific."

Religion—Mormon and London Missionary Society—has taken hold of the island. Lots of churches.

Shell necklaces for buying. And some very unusual prints from old wood blocks made in the days when Samoans were beating mulberry bark into *tapa* cloth.

No restaurants, and the hotel food is somewhat grim.

Samoa has just come out from under a New Zealand protective mandate. It hasn't quite made up its mind whether it wants tourists or not.

This is the world's greatest explosive population, by the way.

New drugs have wiped out the killing malaria and filariasis. And like all Polynesians, Samoans love to have babies.

The money is the Samoan pound, equal to the New Zealand and English pound at $2.80 U.S.

Boy meets girl: He isn't supposed to on this island. But he does.

The Fijis

TEAL flies into Nandi Airport on the opposite end of the island from the Crown Colony capital of Suva.

The Fijians are big, black, bushy-haired, and friendly.

They used to eat people—the last man who came to dinner was a Nantucket whaler.

There is a grasshopper plane service over to Suva.

Or you can take a taxi halfway around the island to the resort of Korolevu.

Korolevu is a tropical resort hotel, made up of *bures*—the thatched native hut. In this case equipped with modern plumbing.

The Pacific washes in becomingly on a palm-fringed shore. The hotel is clean and neat—though a little dull

of an evening. A sort of bowling-ball game is the big event. Once a week, the hotel imports some frizzy-haired Fijians who dance up and down pretending to throw spears at each other in a colorful native way.

The food is quite—well, it's like the Sydney food before the Italians moved into King's Cross. Frightful. They do have a way of cooking over native hardwood charcoal that gives a flavor every backyard barbecue chef would give his crying towel to own.

The wine they opened for me was sour. But in this Australian-operated island, they think you should drink good Australian beer. Wine is plonk, mate.

* * *

Suva is a pleasant town, colored by Fijian police in wraparounds cut at the bottom with pinking shears.

There is a handsome governor's mansion, some nice houses, and a pretty harbor where P & O–Orient and Matson ships anchor on boat day.

The hotel is the Grand Pacific—the GPH throughout the South Pacific.

It has a lovely, cool veranda with everyone in crisp white shorts and bush jackets. When I was there, they ran it like a dormitory. Everybody in bed and lights out at 10 P.M.

Now I hear they have livened things up with a dance on Saturday nights.

An East Indian houseboy wakes you at 6 A.M. with "Tea, master."

If this does not do it, another boy sits outside and beats a wooden drum called a *lali*. This is the call to breakfast. And at the GPH, they run things on schedule.

The money is based on the Australian: $2.24 U.S. to the Fiji pound. Broken up in the English system of half crowns, shillings and pence. Queen Elizabeth on the front and a Fiji turtle on the back.

Imported East Indians run the town business. You can have a bush jacket tailored up in short order.

The language throughout is English, of course.

No health problems. Australian and English doctors available.

The Colonial English feeling is that you dress for dinner.

The food is not much. If there is a good restaurant, I didn't find it. But there are some curry shops. The curry I had at the GPH was not so good.

Boy meets girl: I suppose so. But you've got to *love* that beehive hairdo.

* * *

The drive around the island is not rewarding. Mostly sugar cane—and when you've seen one cane, you've seen them all.

There are some villages you might visit inland. Hunt Travel Agency in Suva could advise you.

For souvenirs, you can buy some excellent tortoise-shell work here.

They also sell a set of gruesome wooden dishes. The kind they used to cook Grandpa in. It was a ceremonial affair. Not *anybody* could just eat anybody.

Chiefs ate people every day. But the common people had to wait until there was a war on and the shop opened up.

At this time, certain delicate portions were cooked and served in appropriate dishes. The one used for serving leg-of-sailor is quite good for a salad bowl.

* * *

The best trip in the Fijis is by the yacht *Blue Lagoon,* captained by Trevor Withers.

The *Blue Lagoon* sleeps 10. It makes a two-day cruise and a four-day cruise down to the primitive Yasawas. The $100 charge includes a ceremonial dish of kava, a peppery root drink, with a native chief. And food and drink on the trip.

These are spectacular islands. Truly native. A voyage-away-from-it-all.

It's popular. You should have plenty of advance reservation.

Tahiti Tours

You can spin around this enchanted island in about five hours, I would guess from driving it once. (It took me about eight, but I stopped off for a little beachcombing for shells.)

There is supposed to be a tour bus. I have never seen it myself and don't know anyone who has ridden it. You can also hire one of the taxi drivers. (There doesn't seem to be any fixed rate on taxis on Tahiti.) If you do, Jimmy in front of Hotel Tahiti, looked to me like an articulate person.

One nice thing about Tahiti drivers: They haven't had enough tourists yet to get the know-it-all, superior attitude that is so infuriating in so many places.

There is also *le truck*—the truck-bus that hauls the majority of Tahiti's people from the districts. It's open-air, wooden seats, cheap and adventurous.

I have used a rental car from Dave Cave at the Hertz agency. Mainly because taxi fares are high and a car is a convenience unless you want to sit in the hotel all day.

At cheaper prices you can rent a scooter.

Or you can go all native and rent a putt-putt motor bicycle. Like the ones you see in coveys every morning, each topped by a Tahitian girl in a print *pareu* with her black hair streaming in the breeze.

Circle Island Tour

Poroi Tours on the waterfront street in Papeete will set this up for you. Or your hotel desk.

This tour (and the side excursions) is a favorite of Mike Costa. Mike handles public relations for TAI, the French jet airline that flies from Paris and makes an attractive turnaround for Americans at Los Angeles.

"Without any great strain and no preparation (other than being dressed in time and making sure your cameras are loaded), one can in a day or, at most two days, see all the major points of interest on Tahiti," Mike wrote me.

(Mike, by the way, says there *is* a chartered bus.)

The guide speaks English—after a fashion. Tahiti hasn't become as efficient in tourism as Hawaii. For which many people are thankful.

* * *

Tours usually open up with a slow drive through Papeete. This is a South Pacific town of 20,000. It is the absolute Paris to every belle shredding coconut out in the Tuamotu coral islands. Look at it that way.

For you it's a sandy little town of overhanging balconies, Chinese frame stores, a great splash of flowers, copra boats tied up at the waterfront, and a bicycle parade of brown girls.

You see the governor's mansion. A few shops and the market place. The cathedral. Anyway, you should come back and just walk around the streets. Early morning is best for the market. And Vaima on the waterfront is where you get your morning coffee.

If you go eastward, the route takes you through the district of Fautaua. Make a note when the guide tells you of the road to the bath of Loti. You may turn off. But if you don't, you might want to come back on your own to see this tropical garden bathing place described in *The Marriage of Loti.*

The tour will take you on to the tomb of King Pomare V, the last king of this paradise. You will also be told that the tomb resembles a bottle of Benedictine, this being Pomare's favorite sauce.

Other people say this is not true. But it makes a good story and no guide will miss telling it to you.

There is a turnoff to Point Venus. In the late 18th century, Captain James Cook came here to observe the transit of Venus across the sun—a matter very important to astronomers. Tahiti was the ringside seat.

It was at this time that the British sailors learned the ratio of iron to island love. They pulled nearly all the nails out of Cook's ship for trade-in values.

The Point is a pretty grove of coconut trees with a black-sand beach.

A mile away is the home of Jean Masson, one of the finest painters in the South Pacific. You have to wade to get there. But I found it worth while even though Masson was not home and I had to look at his work through the windows.

Approaching the Point Venus turnoff, you pass Bounty Bay. This is where Captain Bligh anchored and kept his breadfruit seedlings until the famous mutiny.

If you didn't know it, Bligh was commissioned to bring breadfruit seedlings from Tahiti to the West Indies to feed slaves. The mutiny, described dramatically by Nordhoff and Hall, has been made into two movies.

The canoe used in the Marlon Brando version is now on the lawn at Hotel Tahiti. And practically everybody you see out here was an extra.

James Hall's widow lives on the hill overlooking the bay. She's a charming woman and if you can fix an invitation, she'll no doubt show you the grave where Hall is buried above the ink-blue sea.

The tour follows the coastline. Tahiti is one of the "high" volcanic islands. The interior is small but rugged. Jagged dark-green peaks rise into fluffy clouds that always hang over this type of island.

The low area along the coast is planted with coconuts, breadfruit, papayas, and grapefruit that grow to the size of a basketball.

It gives you a perfect picture of why Tahitians won't get into the Chamber of Commerce spirit and build tourist hotels. The back yard is the free grocery store. And all you have to do is throw a net into the sea for a panful of fish.

You stop halfway around the island for lunch—a really good lunch, which is unusual on Tahiti. The Taravao.

If you are in a great mood for the faraway life, you can make arrangements here to stay on a tiny island off the coast. The proprietor sends a canoe with food and wine each day. You do your own fishing and bring down your own coconuts.

Because preparation of coconuts is difficult, most men who visit the island bring a Tahitian girl along. At least that is what they tell me. Anyway, coconut is hard to open if you don't know how. You can use some help.

Off this narrow part of the island is Tahiti-iti, the little bulge of the island with no roads. You can arrange to get to some parts of it by canoe.

On the westward return trip, the other side of the

island, the scenery is more lush. The road goes through small villages and alongside tropical lagoons.

A stop is made at the Marae of Arahurahu, an ancient sacrificial altar and burial place.

You should be back just in time to see the sun go down in a great shower of gold over the sea and the peaks of the island of Moorea.

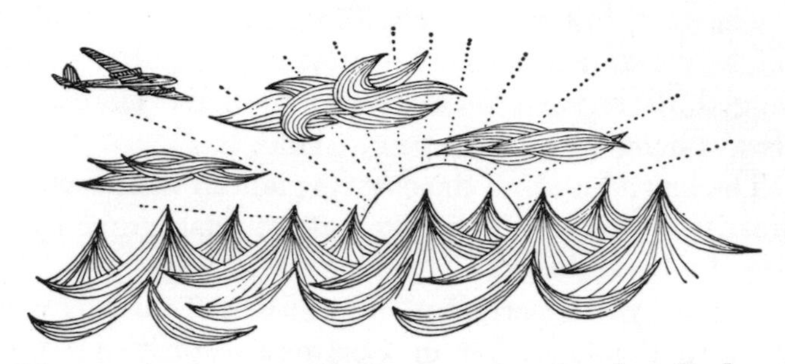

I'd suggest you see this from under the thatched roof at Hotel Tahiti with a chilled Martinique rum punch in hand.

Moorea Tour ($25 for the day, $50 overnight)
Moorea is 12 miles across the channel from Tahiti. The favorite tour over here—bought from any of the water-front agencies—takes you over by boat. Usually loaded with chickens, guitar players, ironware, and other colorful items.

You can stay overnight at a good hotel. Scenic drive around the island and there's a Tahitian dance at night by firelight.

Try to get over when the Matson cruises aren't in town. They run a half-thousand people over. It gets pretty crowded.

Bora Bora Tour ($131 from Tahiti and return for two nights, three days)
The flight by RAI DC–4 to the old American bomber

strip will cost you about $40 round trip. *UNLESS* you have your original airline specifically write Bora Bora on your trip. In addition to your takeoff point to the South Pacific.

It's one of those regulations with airlines. Have them write in Bora Bora at no extra cost and save the four-oh.

Trip takes an hour over an azure sea to the most beautiful island in the South Pacific. Don't plan to sightsee. The only town is Vaitape and it has two Chinese stores and a real Somerset Maugham hotel called Tiare Tahiti—strictly for the adventurous.

The plush hotel is out of town—a $6 taxi ride for six miles. Al Bourgerie will pick you up free.

Hotel Bora Bora has all you want. Turquoise lagoon. All swimming equipment. Good food. Lie on the beach and forget going anywhere.

Tuamotus Tour

The RAI flying boats have recently started flying into the faraway coral atolls of the Dangerous Archipelago.

You sleep in the chief's hut. (And according to all South Seas writers you should be offered the chief's beautiful daughter. The correct drill in these affairs is to say "no thanks" and mutter something about the White Man's Burden. I haven't been out there so I wouldn't know.)

These are coral islands surrounding a lagoon—that's the way coral grows. In diving season, you may see diving for pearl shell. And there's a lot of dried coconut around called copra.

Living is easy. But the RAI schedule changes from time to time. Be sure they don't leave you out there waiting for a passing schooner.

Surely worth the trip.

FARAWAY PLACES

Taipei

The stop on Formosa comes at no extra cost on your round-the-Pacific ticket. You fly it on CAT jet liner between Tokyo and Hong Kong.

Your hotels are:

Grand. A beautiful view of the countryside from this hilltop hostelry. Drive up under a porte-cochère painted Chinese red. It's impressive. Swimming pool and tennis courts. The 53-room extension should be completed now.

The First Hotel is the newest. 133 rooms.

Dragon. Downtown near the CAT office. Small with not much lobby, but the rooms are large and clean and fairly attractive. The hotel keeps a pedicab for your use outside.

For restaurants:

The **Grand Hotel** probably has the best food and definitely the best atmosphere for tourists. Both Western and Chinese cooking.

The **Yu Yuan** for spicy Suchow food. Plain and good for lunch. The proprietor will help you order.

The **Riverside** is on Sueh Yuan Road by the river. Better have your cab wait. They're hard to get out there. You eat outside on the terrace. Pick your food and condiments from a long picnic table. Beef, pork, chicken, wild boar, and venison. The idea is to take it over to the brazier and cook it yourself. But there are waiters to help you if you like.

New Caledonia

The French islands are coming into tourist focus, mainly through efforts of TAI, the French airline, whose planes stop here en route from Australia to the Fijis and Tahiti.

A different people and more French than the Society Islands. Good beaches, and good weather and French cooking, which always helps.

Your hotels:

Lantana is three miles from Noumea town on Anse Vata Beach.

Nouvata Bungalows is just what it says, a bungalow-type hotel. On the beach too.

La Perouse is in town—18 of the rooms have private bath.

Lutetia is a half-mile from town. **Holiday Apartments** is right in town.

There are several good restaurants which mix French with French Colonial cooking—Tahitian raw fish, Indonesian *bemi,* Vietnamese *chowminh,* North African *cous-cous* and *mechoul.*

Try Biarritz on Anse Vata Beach. The Marsupilani on Baie des Citrons beach. La Potinière on Orphilinat Bay. Cyrnos, La Perouse, and Asia in the city.

There is a flying side trip to **Isle of Pines.** One hotel, the **Relais de Kanumera.** Melanesian-style bungalows. Two excellent beaches. Dining room and bar. Swimming, tennis, pedal boats, water skiing, and trips around the island.

Indonesia

The country is making a play for tourists without too much luck because of the political situation in Southeast Asia. BOAC flies into Djakarta. So does Pan American.

Your hotels:

Hotel Indonesia is Pan American's big, modern, air-conditioned place. French, Chinese, or Indonesian food. About 30 shops and four bars. Swimming pool and a splash pool for the kids.

Duta Indonesia is in the center of town. Air-conditioned. Western or Indonesian food. Reasonable rates. Very.

You can fly to **Denpesar, Bali.**

Bali Hotel has 80 double rooms with bath. You pay the double rate even if you're alone. But the price is right. No hot water but you won't need it. Native dances and European or Indonesian food.

Segara Beach Hotel is five miles from Denpesar. Good white-sand beach. Six bungalows on American plan and 25 rooms, all with bath. Beach parties, Bali dancing (with brassières), sailing-canoe rides.

The money in Indonesia is pegged at government levels but there is a black market. And in Hong Kong you can buy at realistic rates. But—there is a tight currency control. Indonesia is the only place I've heard of recently where Customs put on an occasional down-to-the-skin search for illegal incoming currency.

New Guinea

This is for the adventurous. Correspondents I know have gone into Controlled Territory and Uncontrolled Territory where Stone Age men chop you up with stone hatchets. Tourists generally are not on the invitation list.

But you can fly up to Lae on the north coast and be on the edge of primitive mankind. Hard to get to. World War II battlefields. **Hotel Cecil** is partly air-conditioned. Has a swimming pool and Australian beer.

Pitcairn Island

An occasional cruise ship stops off this island where the descendants of the *Bounty* mutineers lead a churchly, isolated life. They canoe out and sell island carvings. Might also be an occasional interisland schooner headed that way. If so, Agence Tahiti Poroi or Tony Bambridge in Papeete would know about it.

Tonga Islands

Occasional service from the Fijis by Fiji Airways. The "hotel" is a converted missionary house. Queen Salote

has a protective treaty with the British. But it is the only independent Polynesian kingdom left. Interesting but not lively.

The Marquesas

Check Agence Poroi or Tony Bambridge in Papeete again. No air service that I could find. (They say flying boats can't land on account of surf and winds.) Copra-trading schooners go in from time to time.

Rapa

By copra schooner from Tahiti to the Austral Islands. You have to have special permission from the French. The word-of-mouth attraction is that Rapa women outnumber men four to one. (The men leave to become seamen.) The *Bounty* mutineers chose this before Pitcairn. They were driven off by natives—the men, not the women.

Tuamotus

RAI flying boats from Papeete go out to the low-lying atolls of the Dangerous Archipelago twice a week now. You overnight on Rangiroa (pop. 822) in the chief's pandanus thatch hut with side boat trips to other islands. Pearl-shell diving is March to June. A day out in these islands and Papeete looks like Paris. It's like landing with Captain Cook.

Korea

Hasn't had many tourists since Uncle Sugar gave us an all-expense-paid trip, good for passage up to the 38th parallel. Seoul financiers have opened a multimillion-dollar multi-hotel operation outside of town at Walker Hill.

The five hotels are based on a luxurious gambling casino plus dormitories for Les Girls in the back of each hotel. (Each is named patriotically for a famous American general.)

Bets on this are that the Army will declare it off limits

to the 50,000 GIs at whom it must be primarily aimed.

If all this appeals to you, there are flights from Tokyo.

AND ANOTHER THING

In the outlying, off-tourist-beat places, carry a supply of everything you might need. (Including toilet paper.) Two outfits—one to wear, one to wash—should be enough. A few emergency pills. Antibiotic and aspirin. A pocketful of dime-store balloons is good. You blow them up for the kids. But be a little careful in very primitive country such as New Guinea. Grown men don't play. And some of these things might look like black magic.

Tobacco is understood all over the Pacific and makes a good present.

Be slow with motions. Our gesture of the hand for "come here" in some countries looks like a threatening gesture.

ONCE MORE AROUND

Hawaii

In the not-so-sleepy paradise of Waikiki, shops stay open nights for the booming tourist trade. The languorous beach boys belong to a union—at least they have some kind of closed corporation.

The languorous tourist rushes from the morning hula lesson to the noon ukulele lesson to the ceremonial luau.

By evening he is exhausted.

* * *

The pressure in Waikiki has pushed numbers of tourists to the outer islands—Kauai, Maui, and the "Big Island" of Hawaii.

The flying time is a half-hour to an hour—pleasant flights over ink-blue seas.

With all its stern concessions to modern progress, the Islands still maintain a great deal of the tropical feeling that charmed Captain Cook, assorted sailors, and Robert Louis Stevenson.

The cooling trade winds blow as if turned on by the Chamber of Commerce.

The lei sellers' huts on Kalakaua Boulevard are a block of ginger fragrance. (There is some talk of prohibiting these colorful stands as detrimental to the modern look of chrome and glass.)

The palm trees (shorn of the budding coconuts which

might knock a tourist on the noggin) rustle in the evening breeze.

The sun falls benevolently on the shoulders of the white-skinned tourist and the brown-skinned native Hawaiian (Chinese, Japanese, Portuguese, Polynesian —whassamalla you, all mix up?).

The pathway to paradise comes at reasonable rates: $250 round trip by air from the Mainland.

The hibiscus blooms vividly on the pathway. The Hawaiian print dresses are excellently designed and very inexpensive.

The *mai tais* are a buck and a half but strong as a wire splice. So who cares what *hoomalimali* these writers put in the papers. Set up one more and let's cut out the *pilikia*.

* * *

The Hawaiian hula is a great tourist attraction and the fiftieth state is very much aware of it. Hula lessons are given in public schools. And the Islands-to-Mainland Matson liners give hula lessons on each voyage.

The professional hula dancers wear grass skirts. (The grass-skirt idea was imported from Samoa.)

It is usually green. The lady wears a green brisket covering.

The step is a sort of sliding dip. It gives the hips an appearance as though you were looking at them from a rolling ship.

The hand movements tell the story. The hand gestures are exact, as though you looked them up in the dictionary.

The hula tells very simple stories:

"A boy meets a girl. They decide to have a picnic. They get on a boat and eat lunch."

The older hulas were extremely suggestive. And if

you are lucky enough to meet an older Hawaiian lady, sometimes she will do one for you.

There is a kind of royalty group in the Islands—descendants of the late 80s, when King David Kalakaua ran an operatic court down at Iolani Palace.

Many of these people retain their titles—Duke and Princess and so on—and generally only turn out for festive occasions like Aloha Week.

If they are alone, one of the older ladies will do one of the old-time hulas. And the Hawaiians sit around and laugh themselves sick.

Naturally, the naughty hulas—they are like burlesque jokes—are not taught to the tourist ladies.

One of the hotel entertainment directors explained:

"If we taught that kind of hula and explained it, the tourists would be insulted. The kind of hula they want to learn is something romantic. Like waving their hands to indicate palm trees. And flying fish and blowing kisses.

"The old-time hula is a little on the blue side."

The major hula taught to the beginning Mainland hula learners is the "Hukilau."

It is a Tin Pan Alley song about a fishing party.

". . . *where the lau lau is the kau kau of the luau. . . .*"

All the ladies indicated with their hands that they were now eating. Their hips revolved like the driving rod on a Mississippi paddle-wheel steamer.

It is an extremely graceful sight—and goes well with banana pancakes and coconut syrup.

"The hula lesson is probably the most entertaining feature of the Hawaiian hotel business," said the entertainment director. "It transports them, makes them a part of the scene.

"Why, just a week ago they were home doing the dishes. And now, look. They're making hand motions like birds flying. Beside the beach at Waikiki!"

Japan

TOKYO

In 1854, Commodore Perry and the U.S. Navy's black ships sailed into Tokyo harbor. They found an antique, thoughtful civilization.

The noble samurai sliced people in half for the slightest breach of etiquette. (The Navy only flogged offenders.)

Rich and poor bathed once a day. (The Navy was lucky if it was once a month.)

The capital supported the glittering, honorable Yoshiwara district. A special drum beat told the Japanese soldier when to go to these pleasure palaces. (The Navy was warned against them. They went anyway.)

* * *

Naturally, both sides tried to change the other. (It is only normal for all of us to civilize each other. With a gun if we have to.)

The results have been excellent. And this year, Japan Tourist Association estimates a quarter of a million Americans will visit the land of cherry blossoms—may even learn to eat with fresh, wooden chopsticks instead of the ugly habit of putting iron forks in their mouths.

"One thing Americans should learn," said a Japanese, "is to call someone to you by waving your hand with the palm down. Not up. When you do it with the palm upward, pulling your hand toward you, it looks like you are making a threatening gesture.

"Besides," he said logically, "the other way *means* 'Come here.' "

"The question of 'yes' and 'no' is extremely difficult for the American," he said.

"Japanese ask their questions so that you are not embarrassed by having to say 'no.'

"Where you would say: 'Would you like more coffee?' the Japanese says: 'You wouldn't like more coffee, would you?'

"In this way, you can say, 'Yes.' Meaning, "Yes, I don't want any more coffee.' "

"But what if I do want more coffee? I *like* coffee," I said.

"We are very sympathetic with your problems in Cuba and Berlin," he said.

* * *

Direct questions are seldom asked in Japan. And even questions about directions are indirect.

When they are answered, the questioner replies with "Is that so? Well, well. Please pardon me."

Business negotiations are almost always handled by a go-between. How could you possibly intimate to a man's face that the price might be too high?

"Face"—reputation and self-respect combined—is so important to Japanese that it causes suicides. You can lose face not only by what *you* do. You can lose face by what somebody does to you. Even by chance of fate.

"A Japanese cannot, for instance, admit inability to do what you would like," said the Japanese. "If you ask a manufacturer to make and deliver an order on a certain date, he feels obligated to say 'yes.'

"If you had used a go-between, he would be able to say that he cannot make it or cannot deliver it."

This unpredictable, direct questioning on the part of Americans has an effect even in department stores.

Clerks stand in a nervous, giggling knot rather than wait on the American. He may ask directly for what he wants. Japanese conversation is loaded with "excuse me." Before anything has happened to cause it.

"This is a natural thing from hundreds of years of rigid etiquette," said the Japanese. "When Commodore Perry deplored the custom of execution for a breach of manners, remember even the Japanese who was executed approved of the system."

"In the old days, if you accidentally slapped me on the back, I would lose face and have to kill myself. You in turn, would be executed. You wouldn't want that to happen, would you?" I asked.

"Yes," said the Japanese. "And again, no."

Nothing upsets Japanese equilibrium like a change of the rigid status between individuals.

Face is lost that can never be recovered. The American is ignorant of Japanese custom. The Japanese cannot advise him—advice and criticism are the same thing.

The complications are endless.

The other day a drunk walked through the train on the Tokyo Express. He clobbered 29 passengers, one after the other. No. 30 he simply threw off the train.

This was unusual. Japanese men get wonderfully loaded. But peacefully.

They do not hit. The relationship between hitter and hittee sets up obligations that are unthinkable.

"Like a person in an accident. Nobody will touch him or even look at him," said Al Ricketts, the *Stars and Stripes* columnist.

"First, you may be obligated to carry on—even into taking care of his family. Then there is *his* obligation to you. Even the victim would rather not get involved."

The unthinking bully-boy of the Express was too ginned to remember. He hit No. 1 while No. 2 watched.

Then he hit No. 2 while No. 3 watched. And so on to No. 30.

That is, 30 men (who could have thrown him up for grabs or at least hit first) sat by and got chewed up one at a time.

"In a disaster like this," said Ricketts, "the Japanese is paralyzed by the implications of involvement. He just sits there and closes his eyes and says to himself: 'I hope it won't happen to me. I hope it won't happen to me.' "

* * *

Reja taimu is the current Japanese worry—"leisure time." (Modern Japan tosses off American phrases like we throw a French *savoir-faire* into a sentence.)

Says *Inside Japan* magazine:

> A local newspaper recently came up with *shokkingu* (shocking) findings: 67.8 *pasento* (per cent) of young *sari-man* (salary-men) interviewed said their aim is to have a pleasant, carefree life.
>
> Only 4.7 per cent said that they aim at contributing to their society.
>
> Actually, *masu komi* (mass communication) and *janari-zumu* (journalism) took the *ridashippu* (leadership) to build the recent *reja bumu* (leisure boom).
>
> It has encouraged the public to indulge in pleasure-seeking during their *supeya taimu* (spare time).
>
> Newspapers and magazines have played up the *reja mudo* (leisure mood) so much so often that some Tokyoites even suffer from *reja noiroze* (leisure neurosis).

Reja taimu is the Japanese cup of tea. Nothing pleases the Japanese like worrying about abstract philosophy. Everybody worries about his *reja mudo*.

Continues *Inside Japan:*

> The Japanese *meka* (maker) is merciless. They use the trend as a *gudo chansu* (good chance). They've vigorously started the summer sales campaign to sell *mota boto* (motor boats) by renaming them *reja boto*.
>
> They are using the *kyacchi furezu* (catch phrase) "Enjoy *supido* (speed) and *suriru* (thrill)!"

The frantic search for ways to fill *reja taimu* makes the hard-working Japanese work twice as hard. Twice as long.

This is an early-to-bed city. Cocktails start at 4 o'clock. Dinner is early. Night clubs are booming at the 9-o'clock show. Dancing is on a curfew of 11:30. And so to bed.

"But now there are bootleg, all-night dancing clubs," Lee Chia told me last night in the Foreign Correspondents Club (and there's a spot that has been in a *reja mudo* for years).

Chia is chief of the Tokyo Bureau of Central News Agency of China. On the side he's a night-life expert and runs *Inside Japan.*

"If the police arrive at a bootleg dance, the waiters rush a couple of table with glasses on them into the center of the floor.

"When the police go away, they pull off the tables and the dancing goes on."

It's a *reja lifu.* But it takes a lot of hard work.

About the first thing the visiting American learns to say in Japan is *ofuro*—"the honorable bath."

If you have an English-speaking maid, she will say: "*Hotu bassu.*" You can get a lot done by adding *u* to an English word.

The honorable bath is so honored that there are enormous pleasure palaces advertised in the papers.

"*Relax and forget your worries! Bath with music! Night clubs! Pretty girls!*"

I must say it takes a little relaxing while the pretty girl scrubs you like a floor.

"You big baby-san. Me little mama-san."

You ain't just a-whistling "Dixie," mama-san!

Tokyo Onsen and a hundred other Tokyo baths cater to the tired businessman.

The decor is gardenlike: The small rooms with a flower arrangement—the tall grass symbolizes heaven, the lower greens the earth. Man is represented as the catalyst between the two in the intermediate blossoms.

The music is usually American jazz.

Drinks are served at the table.

And through this paradise wander the pretty scrub-women. Ready to lead you into the steamy ways of relaxation.

In Japan, Duz doesn't do everything.

This sudsy way of life extends into all Japanese life. (Except in the Western-style Imperial or New Japan. Where the Ugly Americans soap themselves in Western plumbing in the ugliest way imaginable.)

Japanese bathe daily. Between 4 and 7 o'clock.

Bathing in the morning is considered a sybaritic luxury.

"Bass in morning, drink in morning, dance in morning. Pretty soon rich boy, he have no more money," said the Japanese maid, quoting a piece of philosophical verse.

In Japanese hotels, the first thing the maid does is bring you tea and a hot cloth to wipe your face and hands. Then she draws a bath.

The bath (like dining) is supposed to have feminine assistance. At your dinner table, the waitress sits throughout the meal—ready with conversation and the sake bottle.

At one hotel I had a maid who read me the morning papers through the whole soaking process.

"Boy-san love girl-san. No can marry. Both jump in river. Die."

She was a suicide buff. Japanese hit the barbiturate route so often that sleeping pills are the only drugs you need prescriptions for.

The *hotu bassu* requires a ritual. You are scrubbed with soap and towel. (You wash your own face, however. At little taps along the wall.)

The scrubwoman throws water on you. Dipped from the deep *hotu bassu* with a little wooden tub. (You sit on a little wooden stool.)

You then climb in the *hotu bassu* and soak.

The bath is used by other people—that is why you should get all the soap off.

In the hot-springs resorts, the *hotu bassu* is a community affair. A sort of steamed lobby where the guests can sit around and compare travel notes.

It is not only relaxing. It is extremely informative.

In a *hotu bassu* in Atami, I learned things you'd never learn around the whole Hilton hotel chain. Not if you sat in the lobby for a hundred years.

In the warm morning, I checked out of the Japanese hotel. These things are ceremonial and emotional. It is not like paying your bill at a Hilton.

"You go America, you come back soon Japan," said the maid. She dabbed a handkerchief at her eyes because parting is such sweet sorrow. (Did you ever have a desk clerk cry when you checked out?)

There is a little ceremony of present-os. The hotel gives you a present-o. It is usually a handkerchief, for you to cry on when you go.

I made a little present-o of "tea money" to my personal maid.

For a good many days, Yuki-san and I have been thicker than a Reno dealer and a high-roller.

We discuss movies and she teaches me to sing "*Kimigayo,*" the Japanese national anthem.

I know that her favorite movie was *Gone With Window.* Clock Gobble was the star. She regretted nobody sang a song she likes about the South: "O-Blackjo."

She liked Mollon Bu-rand-o in *Wonai Jack.*

I promised to get her a photograph of Mollon Bu-rand-o. And I will, if his press agent will get on the ball.

* * *

In turn, Yuki-san knows I like my *hotu bassu* not too *hotu.* She draws it at 7:30 and I have breakfast at 8: *hamu* and *eggsu* and *hotu cohi.*

She also brings all the morning *shimbuns.* Because she knows I work for shimbuns.

I am required to state what time I will come home each night.

This is not a bed check. Your hotel maid has to wait up until you come home. Things like this haven't happened to me since I was in my teens.

It is quite a strain. And I have to tell people:

"I have to go home now. My maid is waiting up for me."

* * *

I have read Yuki-san's palm. She will marry a rich man and have three children: two boys and one girl. She will have a long life.

Yuki-san advises me that I can get rid of a lot of trouble by sprinkling salt on the floor.

"Suppose man come, you no like. He go. You put salt in door. Make clean."

The same thing can be accomplished with sparks. I let Yuki-san spray me with a few flashes from my lighter before I go out.

Sometimes I get tired of sitting on the floor and I sit on the little two-foot-high table. But not when Yuki-san can see me.

"Sit on table like Japanese say: 'You sit on papa-san's head.' "

My unlucky years were when I was twenty-six and forty-two.

A woman's unluckiest year is thirty-three. I am glad I am not any of these ages.

Yuki-san brings me a fresh *yukata* each day. This is a kimonolike garment of cotton. (You do not wear your clothing in a room.) It folds from left to right. If I crossed it the other way I would be dead.

If Yuki-san came to my funeral, they would have to throw salt on her before she could come back in the house.

At the door, all the maids lined up. They all dabbed their eyes. Heavenly days, it's terrible to be such a heart-breaker!

We all said "*Sayonara.*" (That was a picture we liked, too.)

The maids trotted a few paces after the car, waving their handkerchiefs.

ATAMI

"Atami on Sagami Bay is the Riviera of Japan," said the travel folder. "To soothe your eyes you will be able to gaze upon the colorful tints of mimosa and orange trees.

"And to put your mind at ease, there is the endless emerald-green of the sea embracing our islands."

To this poetic (and true) description let me add:

Atami is a jumping town. Saturday night and every Japanese cat swinging on a chandelier!

The express from Tokyo Central Station rolled an electric hour and a half through Kelly-green fields and dull-brown villages to reach Atami.

The two main streets were bright with neon. And the roadways packed with Japanese vacationers shopping the Coney Island souvenir shops.

They wore clacking wooden *geta* and cool *yukatas*—the kimonolike wraparound in bright cotton prints for men and women.

The most popular souvenirs tell the saddest of stories:

Poor Toby. The Love Pine Tree. And Ohatsu, the long-distance swimming girl, who paddled 14 miles every night for love.

At the Japanese sleep-on-floor Kiunkaku Hotel, they issued me a *yukata,* a hot towel, tea, and a maid with a little English.

"Thisu girl-san see pretty boy-san at shrine. Speaking to him very nice, so, ne? 'What you name? I like marry you.'

"Boy-san say: 'You love me must-o prove. Swim my island every night hundred times. Maybe so marry, ne?'

"Boy-san every night keep fire on beach. Ohatsu can find island. She swim all night see boy-san. Swim all night come back. Long way."

"So they got married and lived happily ever after in a swimming pool?"

"Nevah hoppen," said the maid. "Swim ninety-nine times. *Last* time, light go out. Other boy-san jealous. He fight with Ohatsu boy-san. Push over light.

"Ohatsu see light out. Think boy-san no love her. She die in water. Sad, ne?"

After I dried my tears on the *yukata,* I read the travel folder on Atami.

It says Ohatsu didn't swim. She paddled over in a wooden washtub.

So much for local gossip.

The story of Ohatsu (the island is named Hatsushima in honor of her devotion) is printed on flimsy bath towels sold in souvenir shops.

The Love Pine Tree—also on bath towels—commemorates the tale of poor, but honest, Kan-ichi, who loved rich Omiya. Her papa did not see it that way. The lovers were parted.

" 'Suppose you come Atami, it rain,' Kan-ichi tell Omiya-san," said the maid, " 'that rain my crying.' "

Kan-ichi wept a little last night. Very refreshing.

* * *

The hot springs of Atami squirt out 250,000 gallons of steaming water into the beloved Japanese baths each day. They are part of the great attraction of the town.

Sadly, in 1860, a burst of water scalded Toby, the pet dog of the first British Minister.

He was buried with full Buddhist rites (though it is possible he was Church of England rightfully).

The stone near the main street reads: *Poor Toby.*

Sir Rutherford Alcock was so grateful for the Japanese courtesies that he is said to have negotiated some very favorable treaties for Japan.

* * *

With all this sad background, Atami was bursting with joy. The streets were full. The bars were bursting. And every Japanese had his tea cake.

The Kiunkaku (Rising Clouds Mansion) is owned by Mr. Brilliant Moonlight. He speaks some English. The desk clerk is learning. We have some interesting phone conversations.

I looked up the word *ice* in the dictionary and got on the telephone.

"*Kori.*"

"That," said the desk clerk proudly, "is the Japanese word for ice, sir."

The Kiunkaku Hotel is purely Japanese inn: polished wooden hallways; sliding paper-screen rooms opening on pine tree and fishpond gardens.

The maids wear attractive summer kimonos with the colorful *obi* sash at the back. They pad into the room in mittenlike *tabi*. They sit by the table and serve while we eat.

Leave the room for a few minutes, and they have it completely straightened—fresh ice water, fresh ashtrays, papers picked up and piled.

There is a television hidden by a silk table covering.

Reception is excellent. The favorite Japanese program at present is *Laramie*. "I'm gunna draw on yuh, stranger! Becuz we don't like strangers, stranger!"

It sounds stranger dubbed in Japanese.

"We have seven TV stations," I was told in Tokyo. "The prime time from seven to ten in the evening is completely filled with American Westerns.

"When the TV star Robert Fuller came to Tokyo, thousands and thousands of people came to the airport. It was the biggest reception ever seen."

Most Tokyo sets operate perfectly on inside, rabbit-ear antennas.

"When we first had TV," said the Tokyo man, "everybody had outside antenna. The appearance of antenna on your house gave you great face. And many people put up antenna before they could afford the set.

"Then the government opened its own TV station.

"Now we pay a tax on TV—the collector comes to your house and asks if you have a TV set.

"Immediately most people took down the revealing outside antenna. It is better not to pay the tax than to have the face."

Japanese TV people think the popularity of Westerns lies in the Japanese background of the samurai.

The samurai (like the Western heroes) were warriors of high caliber and touchy about their honor. The slightest mistake in manners was enough for the samurai to haul out his sword and chop you in half.

Some of the varmints even chopped people just to test the edge.

The leave-taking at the Japanese inn is ceremonial.

I called for the honorable bill. We gave the maid a small present-o in a ceremonial gift envelope.

We put on our shoes at the outside doorway.

At the taxi, the maids bowed. The assistant manager bowed. The desk clerk bowed. Mr. Brilliant Moonlight, in view of speaking English, shook hands.

"*Sayonara,*" I said.

"That is the Japanese word for good-by," said the desk clerk, bowing.

SHIMODA

This morning I took $20 worth of taxi out along the Izu Peninsula to question a questionable love affair.

The Japanese legend of the beautiful Okichi and the American diplomat, Townsend Harris, is under considerable fire.

"As far as I am concerned," said Ambassador Dr. Edwin O. Reischauer, "it is purely myth."

This is a good deal like saying Betsy Ross couldn't darn a sock. Or questioning the value of Mom's apple pie in war.

So to press.

Mr. Townsend Harris, his mutton-chop whiskers bristling with indignation at mixed bathing and other Japanese customs, landed August 19, 1856, at the fishing port of Shimoda.

"The lubricity of these people passes belief," he wrote in his journal. "The moment business is over, the one and only subject on which they dare to converse comes up. . . ."

He ordered the first cow slaughtered—a piece of barbarity that shook Buddhist vegetarian Japan. Much as if the Russian ambassador in Washington started eating people.

To appease and calm this awful creature, the governors of Shimoda drafted seventeen-year-old Okichi, a Japanese fortune cookie of great beauty.

Naturally, she fell in love with Mr. Harris.

Her sacrifices have been celebrated in poetry and music. In geisha-house dances and by John Wayne in wide-screen Technicolor.

It is 48 miles from seaside Atami to Shimoda—Japan put the American envoy at the tip of the peninsula, as far as possible from Imperial Tokyo.

The road I should think is in about the same shape as when Harris was here. It takes three rough, bouncing hours. And though I was promised an English-speaking driver, it turned out all he could say was "Sank you."

So we drove in smiling silence. With an occasional "Cigarette?" "Ah, so, sank you."

The temple where Townsend Harris set up consular headquarters is in a grove of trees a mile from the center of Shimoda.

No mention is made of Okichi on the monument erected by the U.S. (There is also a monument to the famous first cow that became steaks.)

But with a dictionary, the lady-guide said Okichi was a first-class geisha. (Other sources say Okichi was a scrubwoman. When Harris found out what she was sent for, he fired her after three days with a burst of proper Bostonian hell-and-damnation.)

This last version puts the skids under the annual Shimoda Festival. It is indignantly denied by Shimoda.

"After all," they say, "Harris-san was human."

* * *

The other temple near the center of Shimoda has a series of paintings of Okichi.

Okichi informed of her fate to be sent to the steak-eater.

She is parted from her true love, Tsurimatsu, who promptly hits the sake bottle.

She falls in love with Harris. Harris goes back to the U.S. Okichi gets on the sauce herself. Becomes a Yokohama hairdresser. Develops high blood pressure. Drowns herself March 27, 1890, near Shimoda.

We found a small Japanese bar near the temple. Unwrapped the box lunches and ordered the big bottle of Kirin beer.

With the dictionary, I got the driver working on the two bar waitresses.

"Harris-san, ne? Okichi-san, ne? American ambassador say not in love."

It was a pretty good effort. The driver nodded vigorously and fell into explosive conversation with the girls. They seemed to reach some conclusion.

He turned back to me and said earnestly: "Sank you."

KAWAGUCHIKO

Added to the summer vacationers at Kawaguchiko are a number of sit-down protesters against U.S. Marine maneuvers on a local firing range. They have built squatters' huts and are determined to leap into the path of the bullets.

The firing range is about the last irritant after the long Occupation.

Said Mr. Ishii, who runs the Fuji View Hotel:

"I spent all the years of the Occupation preventing the Army from painting the woodwork in the hotel. I made many excuses.

"You see all this wood—the great tree beams and uprights—came from the Imperial forest. Many trees were blown down in a great typhoon. We petitioned the Emperor for them.

"We could varnish this wood. But paint could never be removed properly.

"So I made excuses: The weather was too moist. The paint would not dry. Painters were not available. All through the Occupation, it was never painted."

Because it was occupied by the Army, most of the Fuji View Hotel is Western.

It has a Western-style bar and baths. And you eat in a dining room.

The hotel seems generally filled with Japanese, however.

They sit in the dining room in the evening. Handling

knife and fork with something of the same self-conscious pride we show when we pick up chopsticks in a Chinatown restaurant.

This is the Five Lake district. There are rather gentle mountains of pine trees and clouds.

The road up from the coast is half paved, half rough gravel.

"Everything will be paved in time for the Olympics," said the driver.

This is a favorite Japanese saying these days. Whatever is to be done will be done by the 1964 Olympics.

Japan has very few privately owned cars.

The people travel by excellent trains.

People who want cars hire them with a driver.

The responsibility in case of accident—by Japanese high moral conceptions—goes far beyond what you can insure yourself against.

All along the road, cars and motorcycles were stopped at view points while the sightseers waited for the clouds to break over Mount Fuji.

They dismounted and bowed in the direction of Fujisan—the 12,387-foot cone has a spiritual meaning.

Climbing Mount Fuji has tremendous meaning to the Japanese. And one great Tokyo advertising firm has an annual climb—no member of the firm is excepted.

Motorcycles snarled along the roads at high speed. The concept of responsibility has been abandoned by much of Japanese youth—to the great dismay of the Tokyo papers who write editorials about it.

The roads around the lakes were crowded with determined young hikers.

Motorboats roared through the splashes of rain on Lake Kawaguchi.

All it needed was a few bears holding up traffic for handouts and it was Yellowstone all over again.

Hong Kong

The Luk Kwok Hotel is in the Wanchai dock area of Hong Kong. As everyone knows, it is the setting for *The World of Suzie Wong.*

A few years ago, the Luk Kwok management became aware that a number of tourists were strangely interested in a girl named Suzie Wong. It apparently amazed them because they could not remember any Suzie Wong.

"Maybe so girl go China side," the mama-san told me when I asked about it.

After William Holden's picture was released, the hotel got the idea. They air-conditioned the rooms. They put in a Western Cactus Room—saddles and sirloins and I-wanna-go-back-to-Laredo music sung by Chinese cowboys.

Business is excellent. If the management does not have Suzie Wong, they have an entertaining story.

"Mr. Mason he sit there," said the bar girl. "He chow-fan man. Like eat chow-fan. Busy man. Sit and eat and write."

Richard Mason, the author of the book.

The Hong Kong *Standard* recently rediscovered Suzie.

Her name, they said, is Wong Yuet-law and she still lives in the Wanchai area. She is twenty-seven. She has had seven children; five of them were given away because she could not support them.

"She recalls vividly at the time of Mason's departure accompanying him to the airport," said the *Standard.*

The *Standard* also says that Mason promised to return and help her if his book made money. And so he did a year ago. But Suzie didn't live there any more.

Suzie was doing a six-month jolt in Laichichok, where they send drug addicts from the Colony.

The story winds up on a note of hope:

"Now that she is finished with drugs, she is facing life with fresh vigor and she hopes that Mason will revisit her. . . ."

A number of "Suzie Wongs" have also sprung up in Hong Kong's dance palaces—Tennochy, the Oriental, the Happy Bar, the Venus Inn.

Three years ago, Tennochy had one Suzie Wong. (It was quite accidental. Suzie had never heard of the book.)

Now nearly all bars have an authentic Suzie Wong.

However, there is only one authentic Luk Kwok Hotel. It is owned by Jimmy Wu, a bustling Cantonese who also owns the plush Maxim's night club and the State, the Royal, and the Queen's theaters—all of them currently showing *The World of Suzie Wong.*

The bar (where Mr. Mason wrote his productive novel) is about the same. The mama-san. The girls in slit-skirt *cheongsams.* A colorful sprinkling of British and American sailors—and a colorful flow of goggle-eyed lady tourists.

* * *

It has been raining for a week in Hong Kong. A gray, warm rain. Soggy clouds were lying up on the Peak. And the red rickshaws at the Star Ferry wore brown canvas side curtains.

There was a car waiting for me at the dock and flowers from Original Jimmy Chen in my room.

This gives me big face. About the most important thing in the Far East is face—a combination of pride, reputation, and status symbols. And most of us would rather appear in public without pants than without face.

"I go to airport and meet your friends you send to me. I give you plenty face," said Mimi Lau.

Mimi is a doll-size newspaper girl. She knows everybody who has ever been to Hong Kong.

"Admirals, President Kennedy, Lady Bird Johnson—all people I interview," said Mimi.

Mimi's biggest face came from her divorce.

She objected to her husband's concubine or "small wife," a custom accepted by most Chinese but not by Mimi Lau.

She divorced her husband and gave him a new concubine.

"Like going-away present," said Mimi.

Since a brand-new concubine (with white sidewalls and radio) costs about $6000 Hong Kong, this gave Mimi face that has lasted to this day.

"Show I don't care," said Mimi. "Also make old concubine very mad."

Face is also maintained by health. We were having dinner at Tin Heung Lau—a lavish, rococo place where "beggar's chicken" is the specialty.

As a side order, Miss Lau was chopsticking Nutri-Bio pills.

"Mr. Bob Cummings give to me," she said. "You know, television and movie star. He take them *all* time."

"Why did he give them to you, Mimi?"

"He want to give me present. He say, 'Mimi, you take these pills, you feel good all time.' "

"Do you feel good all the time, Mimi?"

Mimi said the pills gave her an orbit-bounce. And—

"Everybody want these pills, too. But cannot buy here. Only in Beverly Hills. These pills give big face."

We give each other face. A cable is important and therefore face. My room boy would not think of bringing a cable without announcing it in a loud voice.

"Cablegram come."

This gives me more face than the man next door who only receives letters.

Being my room boy gives the room boy face.

This is a peculiar custom and amuses the American tourist no end.

He goes home with a smile on his face and buys an enormous car with enormous tail fins.

Singapore

Singapore is a wonderfully tropical British colonial island. The dinner music has that Strauss-waltz sweep you hear in the dreary hotels of Piccadilly and Mayfair.

Breakfast is not available until the British hour of 7:30. The coffeepot handle is too hot to touch. The toast comes in the delightful silver toast rack—a device designed to refrigerate it.

The famous Raffles Hotel is a rambling white frame building with a British-tailored tropical courtyard of royal palms and lush banana plants.

While Japanese guns boomed on the boulevards, the

Raffles held stiffly to an officers-only, jackets-will-be-worn-by-gentlemen policy each evening.

General Yamashita, the "Tiger of Malaya," held his military conferences in the lounge. (Where British General Percival had held some of his.)

And in the warm evenings, Malaya rubber planters take their stengahs and Pimm's cups and worry about America's tin policy.

And the sun never sets on the English flag.

* * *

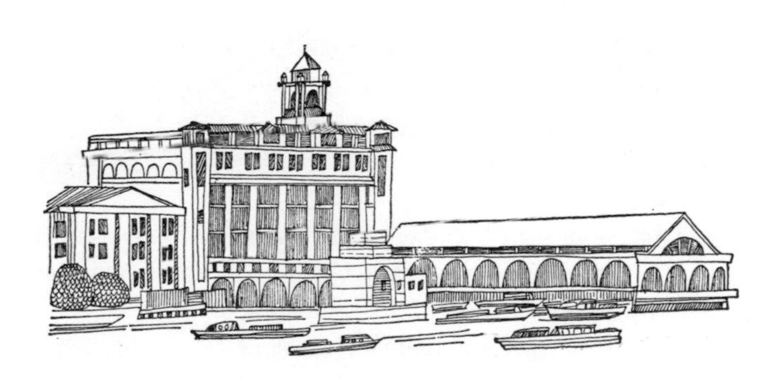

The fringes of Typhoon Pamela are sweeping over Singapore this morning. A sloshing rain is whipping the tall, plumed pencils of royal palms. The cobra charmers in front of the stately Raffles have gathered up their serpents and gone to cover.

I will live to be eighty-two years old.

I am stubborn but charming.

I should watch my liver. (Watch out, liver. Big Brother is watching you!)

Two years from now I will be rich.

That is the morning line from Mr. Lim Sing Cheong. Insurance people and my Money Man can lay odds accordingly.

Mr. Lim reads the future like you and I read a newspaper.

He reads the headlines and the comics. The editorials in my hand and the classified ads.

He is a Chinese mitt reader.

Mr. Lim works in a T shirt. His office is on a rickety balcony overlooking a street full of drying laundry.

The rich, ripe smells of Singapore drift up to Mr. Lim's abode.

And we hear the future to the wailing five-note scale of a Chinese love song.

"Velly good," said Mr. Lim, bending my thumb to see if it would break off. It didn't. "Velly, velly good," he said.

That is the extent of Mr. Lim's English. We operate with an interpreter.

"Mr. Lim says you are jolly stubborn," said the interpreter. He was an Indian from the High Street bazaars with a British accent.

"But he says you are usually correct, therefore it is good to be that way."

"What does Mr. Lim see in the ruddy future, old boy?"

"Mr. Lim says you will live to be eighty-two. The age of forty-three was bad for you. Be careful the year you are sixty-one.

"You are restless and know all parts of the world.

"You are successful in love–" Mr. Lim dropped his eyes delicately.

"Do not drink too much. Your liver will suffer."

Mr. Lim traced some lines on my hand with a pencil point and spoke admiringly to the interpreter.

"Mr. Lim wishes he had your fortune. Your business prospers. But within two years you will be rich beyond all you imagine.

"Your wealth comes by water." (Aristotle Onassis move over.)

Mr. Lim said I would have three children.

He said I was healthy. This confirms my medic, who told me, "I wish I had your arteries."

He gazed on my money line with approval. Like my banker does on my account sheet when my payments are up to date.

"Mr. Lim says many typhoons in your life. Now it will all be jolly good sailing."

* * *

This is pleasant news. When the typhoons sweep tropical Singapore. When the thunder rolls and the rain pounds on the walls.

Outside the door at the Raffles, a turbaned snake charmer is blowing a few notes on a pipe. The cobra comes out of the basket and does a little snaky rock 'n' roll.

I do not go near the snake charmer and the cobra.

I intend to die at eighty-two. Rich and respected.

That cobra might bite me in the liver.

Bangkok

The most interesting recent event in Bangkok was an American cinema company making *The Ugly American* here.

You will remember the book: There were a number of pretty Americans overseas—ambassadors, congressmen, and such. They were pretty to look at. But they were ugly as a monster picture on the inside.

They did not invite the natives to cocktails. (The

Russian envoys were throwing vodka hi-de-ho every night.)

They behaved in the most ugly country-club sort of way. And all of us at home in the country clubs were heartily ashamed of them.

The ugly American was only ugly to look at. Ooh, was he ugly! But he was polite as butter to the natives.

And anyone could plainly see he was Grade-A handsome inside.

This book became a best-seller. It sold wonderfully in Europe—Europeans are delighted to see American authors razor hell out of their diplomats.

* * *

I flew in from Hong Kong on Pan American's time-chasing Flight One around the world. (Because of jet speed and time changes, the daily flight leaves San Francisco at 9:30 in the morning and arrives at Bangkok at 11. Having stopped at Tokyo and Hong Kong.)

It is a rather ugly city with beautiful temples.

"*Su-wa-dee*," said the lady from the tourist bureau. "Which is the Thai way of saying 'Hello, good-by, good morning and good night.' What do you wish to see in Bangkok?"

"I wish to see temple dancing girls," I said in the ugliest way possible. "The ones that twist their necks thisaway and thataway. And wear cone hats with the gold antenna on top."

The lady said the classic Siamese dance was given several nights a week. It is given in the Ambassador night club in the Erawan Hotel.

"Reservations may be made at the hotel desk. It is a great favorite with the Americans."

She drove us on a little sightseeing tour. She said the

Thais are very active Buddhists. Some of the main shrines of the religion are in Bangkok.

The temples are very ornate. They are sandwiched in between very shacky-looking stores in the main business district. Bangkok has a 40-per-cent Chinese population and the Chinese seem to have most of the business buttoned up.

* * *

Twenty-three international airlines fly into Bangkok's Don Muang airport—from Pan American 707s and BOAC Comet IVs to Malayan Airways DC–3s flying down to Penang and Kuala Lumpur.

They unload a fair amount of tourists. Most of them have seen *Anna and the King of Siam* and realize they are in the mysterious land of sacred white elephants, dancing girls, and Siamese cats.

They are in the mood to be romanced—and they soon are.

"That will be ten baht, sir," said the Thai taxi driver. He had soulful black eyes. But he had not dropped the flag on the meter.

(The money of Thailand is the tical—20 to the U.S. $1. For some confusing reason the tical is then known as a baht.)

Since the ride had only been three blocks, I thought 10 baht might be high. But the doorman at the Oriental Hotel assured me it was quite right.

I took another taxi for 20 blocks.

"Ten baht, sir," said the driver.

I took a ride for two miles—10 baht.

"The meter is something new in Bangkok," said Darrell Berrigan, who runs the Bangkok *World.*

"It is the custom here to bargain taxi fares. The drivers resent the meter. It takes all the fun out of life."

Berrigan said he had checked and found that the meter charge from office to his house was 11 baht.

"But I bargain it at 8 baht. Sometimes I argue the other way. I tell the driver, 'Look, if you turn on the meter you will get 11 baht. But you bargain and only get 8.' They still prefer the bargain."

It is quite possible that the Bangkok drivers can afford this luxury. For the tourists have no idea what the rates should be.

They simply ride and ask: "How much is it?"

Such graciousness on the part of the Thai gods cannot be overlooked by the Thai drivers. And they make the most of it.

* * *

The most popular (and cheapest) taxi is a three-wheel motor surrey with a fringe on top.

It has two wide seats in back and one seat by the driver.

It is steered by a handlebar arrangement—though the driver sits inside. There are no doors and no windows. Only a canvas top and a refreshing breeze.

There seem to be two types: the Mazor, made in Hiroshima, and another Japanese model called the Daibutsu Midget. The drivers rent from a central agency.

These taxis are still unmetered and are therefore a joy to their renters.

Prices all along the Bangkok tourist route are raised in a flattering way.

Cigarettes that sell for 45 cents downtown are 60 cents in the hotels.

Local beer is 60 cents a bottle. And a fairly normal hotel dinner can run $20.

It is admitted that the Thais do not pay anything like this amount for living costs. But East and West are sharply split here—by economics, by language barrier, and (I suspect) a number of ways of looking at things.

Taxis, however, are the same the whole world over.

I took a cab for nearly an hour.

"Ten baht," said the driver. "Three," I said. "Five, sir," said the driver. And so we settled—at four baht.

Australia

Australia, as any schoolchild knows, is the home of the kangaroo, the cuddly koala bear, the sly grog shop, and the two-up school.

Nothing delights the Australian more than betting.

For this reason, Australians pour pounds into the race tracks, which offer more exciting ways to lose money than the field on a Las Vegas crap table.

The tracks offer totalizer betting—odds are changed according to the favored betting. They also offer a wonderfully colorful set of independent bookmakers.

The bookmakers' odds change, too. But, if you bet before the odds shorten, you win at the price originally given.

"Naturally," said the Australian journalist, "many people cannot get to the tracks. For these we have the S.P. [starting price] shops.

"In the United States you would call them bookies."

The S.P. shops are against the law. Like the U.S. the police harry them constantly. And, like the U.S., they spring up again, hopeful and eternal.

"But no doubt the most popular game is two-up."

This remarkably simple gambling game is carried on in "two-up schools"—also raided by police.

"You throw two coins in the air," the journalist explained.

"If they come down heads you win. A heads and tails is no game. Both tails, you lose.

"You place your bet and you are 'set'—you would call it covered—by other players. The setting is done by the 'boxer'—a dealer, you'd say."

The first win of the two coins must stand. That is, you let the bet lie. You cannot pull down the winnings until after the second win.

Since few players put up enough money to cover all bets, you are "set" by as many players as you can handle. The others bet among themselves. That you do or you don't.

The odds are quite even. And the house makes its money by taking a small percentage.

* * *

Australian early-closing liquor laws produce "the sly grog shop." An after-hours speakeasy that brings nostalgic tears to the eyes of aging Americans.

The sly grog shop operates in traditional speakeasy fashion: The cautious knock on the door. The peek through the judas. "Alfred sent me." "Right you are."

(It is my opinion that Australians make these laws for the very joy of confounding them.)

The laws vary from state to state. Sydney opens at 10 in the morning. Closes from 6:30 to 7:30. Opens again until 10.

Melbourne closes down at 6.

Bonafide travelers may get a drink. By driving 30 miles you are a traveler—a conception that has put up a string of roaring roadhouses, all exactly 30 miles from Sydney.

New Zealand

Spring has come to Auckland's 450,000 quick-frozen inhabitants—a matter of chilly opinion, but that is theirs.

All over New Zealand, they opened the windows and doors. And they let the cold, cold wind come blowing in.

"Spring is here," said the Customs inspector at the airport.

He said it firmly. As though it had just been passed into law.

"There is no time of the year so lovely as spring," said the lady at the desk of the Great Northern Hotel.

I went up to the room, closed the windows and put on two coats. I began reading *New Zealand Facts and Figures.*

"Except for the native Maoris, most of our 2½ million people are of Anglo-Saxon descent. . . ."

This explains a good deal. Nobody believes in the calendar like the English. When the date reads "spring," the English put off their top coats even if it is snowing outside.

* * *

Medical service is partly paid by the government. There is a strong social-security system, a bonus weekly payment for every child in the house, and very adequate old-age pensions.

When New Zealanders speak of their "welfare state," they do so with pride.

The road from Auckland to Wairakei runs along the Waikato River for five driving hours.

It is pretty, rolling country. Green with New Zealand spring grass and white with little clouds of New Zealand lambs. They ran up and down the green-velvet hills. And ran back to their mamas and drank their milk like good little lambs should.

"Along this river—it's the biggest in New Zealand—the Maoris and the English had a number of battles," said Peter Smythe of the tourist bureau.

He was practically worn out trying to show me the country in three days.

"Who won?"

"The English won," said Peter. "But now the Maoris and the New Zealanders of European descent are completely equal. Politically, socially, economically."

Before this occurred, the Maoris, who were native Polynesians, fought a number of bloody battles for equality.

The Maoris were the only Polynesians who ate people.

Therefore, victories were not only a matter of pride. They went on the Diners' Club card as well.

* * *

The hotel at Wairakei is government-operated—a chain of such hotels worked on a sort of lease basis in the welfare-state economy.

It pipes hot water from the steamy field. (Somehow it ran out of hot water the other morning. I don't see how.)

Tahiti

A modest survey (and modesty forbids my naming the surveyor) shows that when most people think of Tahiti, they think of love.

This is only natural. So many writers have written about the ever-loving Tahitians that the islanders have come to believe it themselves.

"Tahiti, c'est un paradis," sighed the bartender at Les Tropiques.

And I thought if this isn't the ever-loving end. When even the natives start firing the clichés at you.

This is in no way to bum-rap love or the loving Tahitians. (Bless your soul, ma'am. We do not make war on women.)

However, things are not as frisky as when Captain Cook's jolly tars discovered the ratio of kisses to iron nails.

"The fact is," said a friend of mine who lives on Tahiti, "the American male tourist comes down here preconditioned: He expects to have beautiful Polynesian chicks climbing him like a coco palm.

"The place he meets girls is at Quinn's.

"Pretty soon he is going around starry-eyed with something he wouldn't drag out on a dark night in the States."

This type is known to the French government as the banana tourist—"He has never seen a banana growing before and eats the first one off the tree."

They would like to discourage this idea of Tahiti. A number of local American residents have started fishing clubs and other wholesome activities to encourage gentlemen to bring their wives to Tahiti.

The airlines are particularly enthusiastic about this idea. And the local managers of South Pacific Air Lines,

the French TAI, and the New Zealand TEAL fish faithfully on week ends for marlin.

If business is good when you haul men tourists, it is twice as good if you bring their wives.

However, it is hard to cry down the juicy writings of Melville and Loti and the hibiscus-yum-yum paintings of Gauguin.

The great worry of the French Colonial government of French Polynesia is how to get tourist money without getting the tourist with it.

An American living on Tahiti said: "What the French would like is to have only five American millionaires come here each year. And each one spend a million dollars."

The major income of the 110 islands is phosphate from the island of Makatea. This brings roughly $1.25 million to run the islands and service 80,000 people.

"It is also the last paradise of the French petty official," said the American. "France loses money on these islands now. When the phosphate is exhausted—the estimate is fifteen years—tourists are the best source of income.

"But if tourists increase to make the islands important, then they will become a department of France, not a colony. And there goes the French official's job."

The Colonial government makes it very difficult for foreign capital or foreigners to operate.

Only a few Americans who have come here to invest money are staying.

Americans who buy homes may stay six months. Then they must leave and cannot come back for six months.

Foreigners are only permitted to work if it is proved (to the satisfaction of the government) that nobody else can do the work.

The American-operated Iaorana Villa put in a couple of guitar players without a formal permit. It has been banned forever from having an orchestra.

The $600,000 Hotel Tahiti (owned by Spencer Weaver of Honolulu) was threatened with closing because an orchestra leader made an announcement first in English rather than French.

In one exhaustive campaign, all signs in English were taken out unless the French equivalent was also shown.

This involved removing Pan American Airways calendars from schools.

Reflector signs on bicycles reading SPAL (South Pacific Air Lines) were ordered taken off.

A restaurant menu had to be reprinted entirely. It had English on one side and French on the other. But they had used the word *toast* on both sides.

The French said it should have been *pain grillé.*

The tourist is welcome. And the shorter time he stays, the more welcome he is.

"That is the reason they only let you stay six months," said the American. "The French reason that a tourist spends most of his money in the first few weeks. At the end of six months, he is no longer a tourist. He has geared his spending to the island economy and is no longer an asset."

The main tourist the French do not want is the *touriste banane*—the banana tourist.

Economical, short-money tourists are banana tourists.

Although wages are an average $2.50 for labor, the tourist route is fairly high. About $50 a day per couple.

* * *

One of the nice things that has not been changed about Tahiti: They do not expect you to be an Ugly American.

"I doubt if any Tahitian has read the book *The Ugly*

American," said Ralph Varady. Mr. Varady is the author of *Many Lagoons*.

The Ugly American was a best-seller in the overseas market. They made a movie of it in Bangkok. And many people overseas now look at visiting Americans to see how gross and ugly we will be.

Mr. Varady said the Hollywood crew making *Mutiny on the Bounty* turned out to have only a normal percentage of Uglies.

"Many of them were nice-enough people. But let's face it. Some Hollywood gripmen are not our best exports.

"These people are used to a good deal of Hollywood flash and they spent a lot of money. Money does not buy the same thing in Tahiti. But they could not understand that."

It has long been a custom in Tahiti not to tip. Tipping offends the Tahitian idea of hospitality and there are signs at the airport: *No tipping in Tahiti.*

Most people entering the airport do not read the sign. Consequently, they tip the Tahitian porters. This word has gone around. And a number of Ugly Tahitians have got the porter jobs at the airport. They make a good deal of Hinano beer money.

There are also visiting Uglies who just *like* to tip. A lady from Missouri—"Ah'm fum Mizzou," she said—told Varady:

"Ah don't cayah what the custom is 'round heah, Mistuh Va'ady. Ah'm gonna give that girl a nice, fat tip jus' like we do in Mizzou."

The lady would have done better to go down to Papeete and buy the room girl three meters of cotton pineapple print for a *pareu.*

"Don't tip the cocktail waitress," Varady advised. "Ask her to dance once in a while."

* * *

Varady said he studied the *Mutiny on the Bounty* impact on the islands and came to a conclusion that

"If it had been any other sort of group—say a bunch of dentists or insurance men, the results would have been the same. It was not just because they were Hollywood people."

The *Mutiny on the Bounty* people brought a crew of 127 to Tahiti. At that time there were 150 hotel beds on the island.

"Naturally, a lot of the men took up with the island *wahines* and began renting houses. They raised the price of a five-thousand-franc house to fifteen or seventeen thousand." (The Pacific franc runs 88 to 90 to $1 U.S.)

He said the company was very careful about upsetting the economy. They learned that the daily labor rate was 200 francs. They paid 300.

"But only because people had to come from all over Tahiti for the mob scenes. Where Tahiti welcomes Captain Bligh and the *Bounty*."

It did cause a problem with the local banks when they had to cash 3000 checks for 300 francs each.

"They ran out of hundred-franc notes and had to fly in a special load."

* * *

The best way to cure lumbago (said H. W. Camerlynck of Tahiti) is a Persian method.

"They stretch you on the sand and a girl—she is trained in the work—puts one foot on your neck and the other in the small of your back. She pushes her feet in opposite directions and it stretches you. Absolute cure."

This cured M. Camerlynck's lumbago. He has found nothing to cure his Tahitian headache.

M. Camerlynck is in the booming hotel business of Tahiti.

He recently opened the luxurious Hotel Taaone, a few kilometers from the little town of Papeete, the Paris of the South Pacific. (*Life* cut up this town—"dirty, etc." I think they were out of their ever-loving minds.)

"There are difficulties in all hotel operations," sighed M. Camerlynck. "But here in Tahiti they are unusual."

When they were building the Hotel Taaone, Camerlynck cornered all the available matting called pandanus—a leaf from a palmlike tree.

"The best pandanus comes from Bora Bora in the Islands-under-the-Wind. They dry it better and it lasts about eight years on the roof. The island of Moorea pandanus last only six years.

"Here on Tahiti, they don't weave pandanus. Only coconut, which is floor matting."

M. Camerlynck said he got all the prime Bora Bora pandanus. Then he lent some to another hotel builder.

"Now," said Camerlynck unhappily, "he is paying me back in Moorea pandanus instead of Bora Bora pandanus. There is no Bora Bora pandanus available. But still. . . ."

Robert Fraser of San Francisco said it was true that the French Colonial government has some very strict rules on foreign investments. But . . .

"Actually, a lot of complaints against the government rules here are because the hotel builders are a little on the amateur side.

"Why, they only require fourteen permits here. In San Francisco, we have to get thirty permits. And we figure at least two months to get all our papers through City Hall."

The Hotel Taaone is on a black-sand beach. (If you don't have a tan, it makes you look awfully white.)

The *maître d'hôtel* comes from the Tour d'Argent in Paris. The chef is from France. In accordance with Tahiti regulations, a number of other employees are French.

"Part of our employment contracts provide that we have to send them back to France for a month's vacation each year and pay *all* expenses—even in France," said Fraser. "That's why prices are high here."

(Island hotel prices run about $20 a day. Island labor hires out for $2.50 a day.)

* * *

Fraser would like to put a quota system on tourists—there are only 350 hotel beds on the island. He has a luxury hotel on Bora Bora, an hour and a half by flying boat from Papeete.

The airlines—South Pacific Air Lines and the French

TAI—naturally do not want any quota. They want to fill their planes.

The French government would be pleased to put tourists on quota. But they are faced with that dwindling supply of phosphate.

M. Camerlynck said this conflict of interest and practical economy is the headache of the islands. Not to be cured by stretching the back.

On the other hand, "A girl standing on your back really does cure lumbago. I think it could be taught to the Tahitian girls. And this black sand is perfect. It gives an excellent base."

Bora Bora

The RAI flying boat leaves Tahiti three times a week for Bora Bora in the Îles-sous-le-Vent—the Islands-under-the-Wind.

It is an hour-and-a-half flight. Around the sapphire shoal waters of the island of Moorea. Across a painter's blue sea to the island of Raiatea. And then into the turquoise lagoon at Bora Bora.

The new Hotel Bora Bora (owned by Robert Fraser) is run by Al Bourgerie—he used to run Les Tropiques at Tahiti.

"One of the advantages of a hotel like this," said Bourgerie, "is that we get to train our help well. We don't have other hotels stealing our people."

Even with no competition, Bourgerie has the same natural problem that plagues the hotels of Tahiti: Polynesian paralysis. This is a thing the islanders have long been used to. It attacks the newcomer as well—you sit down and don't want to get up and go to work.

Bora Bora has 2000 people with nothing to spend money on.

"It is pretty hard to convince anyone to work when he can pick breadfruit and bananas and coconut out of his front yard. And the sea is full of fish," said Bourgerie.

As an example, he pointed out the fishing party in the lagoon. About 20 boats were moving in a half-circle toward a little sand spit.

In the center pirogue, a brown, brawny Polynesian was throwing a rock in the water. "To frighten the fish ahead," said Bourgerie.

The rock was tied to a rope. The fisherman threw it in the water—clunk! He pulled it out and threw it in again—clunk!

On the shore, the chief of the fishing party chanted instructions. And the circle grew smaller.

"Now watch this," said Bourgerie. "This is why it's hard to keep hotel help in French Polynesia."

Two fishermen in the end boats jumped off on the

sand *motu*. They sealed the ends of the underwater net to the beach.

The rest of the fishermen pulled up the net and dumped about 200 fat tuna into the center.

"There's enough to feed the families for a week," said Bourgerie. "All the other food grows naturally. You don't have to plant it. Just pick it."

The American and French hotel people would like to import help—"One Japanese does the work of three Polynesians." But the French Colonial government is absolutely against it.

There are 7800 Chinese in Papeete, many of them island-born. But only 750 are citizens. Even native-born Chinese, who go to visit in China, have a hard time getting back into the islands.

Bora Bora is a small but spectacular island. It rises to jagged peaks that are continually spiked into fluffy clouds.

The breeze bends the coco palms. A mask and snorkel gives you a view of rainbow-striped fish. The food is excellent, the wine is from France. And the girls of Bora Bora are famous throughout the 112 islands as the prettiest and the best hula dancers.

The last paradise.

The Fijis

There seems to be some question as to who was the last man eaten in the Fiji Islands.

"It was a Nantucket whaler," said the TEAL representative at Suva.

We were sitting on the broad veranda of the old, staid Grand Pacific Hotel—the GPH, as it is known throughout the South Pacific.

"As a matter of fact, I've talked to a chap out in the hills here who got a piece of the whaler."

He said the diner was a small boy at the time. He got the thumbs, which in Fiji at that time was something like getting the neck of the chicken.

The books say it was a missionary named Baker. No address, vital statistics, or types of sauce given.

There is a story that they also tried to eat his boots. But had to give up. One of the chiefs broke his tooth on a nail.

This is no doubt a press agent's embellishment.

The Fijians ate people for many years. You can buy replicas of the carved wooden platters used for serving various cuts. By 1860, the date the Reverend Baker came to dinner, they were certainly sophisticated enough diners not to break their teeth on boots.

The Fijis are some 300 islands. Hardly any tourists get anywhere except to Viti Levu, the island of Nandi Airport, and the Crown Colony capital of Suva.

"The Fijians got the international reputation as cannibals because they look the part," said the TEAL man. "Though heaven knows the Maoris down in New Zealand were just as good trenchermen."

"Actually, they are the happiest, most friendly chaps you'd want to meet."

A Fiji boy in a white wraparound skirt, jagged from being cut with pinking shears at the bottom, brought another king-size bottle of Scotch beer.

He gave me a happy, friendly smile. He had teeth like sugar loaves. I was glad to meet him on the porch of the GPH rather than at dinner.

* * *

"Do I think anybody has been eaten ex-officio, as you might say? Well, I doubt it. The law is very strict about it. Absolutely against it.

"Can't have chaps going about eating other chappies, now can you?

"Still, the French outlaw eating dogs in the Society Islands. Yet dog was a standard product in Polynesia. Not much protein except fish. Why, the Maoris brought dogs into New Zealand with them. Extinct now like the moa bird.

"Absolutely ate them into oblivion.

"Still, tastes change. And Fijians today would prefer canned sardines, I imagine. Of course, you can't keep your eye on everything and some strange things happen out in the primitive outer islands."

Among odd things, he said the best fire-walkers in the South Pacific come from the Fiji Islands.

"The main ones are from an island spelled B-E-Q-A

but pronounced like Mbengga. Sawau tribesmen who live in the four villages on the windward side.

"Now they dig a circular pit about fifteen feet in diameter. They line it with river stones and build a log fire in it—burn it for about twelve hours.

"At the correct time, about twelve of these chappies just walk into the red-hot coals as cool as you might saunter down Queen's Street. Examine them afterward and they'll never show a blister.

"I'll admit that going barefoot all your life puts a sole on you like a hunting boot. But still——"

Another curious thing, he said. "The grass anklets they wear don't even scorch. But if you threw a handkerchief in that fire it'd go up *poof!*

"But for eating people still, well, I rather think not."

The Fiji boy gave me a friendly, toothy smile. And a big happy wink.

* * *

The Fiji beach resort of Korolevu is most popular with tourists. It lies four hours by rough road—halfway between the Crown Colony capital of Suva and the crossroads airport at Nandi.

It is a pleasant long stretch of palm-fringed beach. Coral and sharks make it chancy for swimming. But the sun is bright and the sea is water-color blue.

There is a certain British stiffness. The food is fair—it could be improved tremendously. Fijians cook on eight kinds of charcoal which give a flavor we cannot duplicate in our barbecues no matter how much applewood and sassafras we use.

The guests sleep in Fijian grass shacks called *bures.*

They have been equipped with modern plumbing and mosquito nets and the sea breeze makes them very comfortable.

"You should go sometime to Koro and see them call the turtles," said Don Lane from the Fiji Visitors' Bureau. (Tourist bureau people always try to send you somewhere else, I find.)

"The men of the village dress in a certain way on certain days—they put on ceremonial wreaths of flowers. There are also other ceremonies in advance, quite secret.

"One thing about all South Pacific ceremonies, they usually involve staying away from women and coconuts. This is very difficult in the South Pacific. We don't have supermarkets or TV as replacements.

"Anyway, they perform their ceremonies. And they call the giant turtles.

"You can hardly believe this unless you see it. But dozens of these turtles—they're as big as a dinner table, you know—rise from the sea and swim to the land.

"The natives turn them on their backs and, eventually, eat them. Quite delicious, turtle steak."

On another of the 300 islands (about 100 are populated and most are as primitive as in the days when Fijians were serving boiled New England dinners) the women call the turtles.

"The women wade into the water from the island of Kadavu—quite nude you know except for a flower crown. It probably has some interesting sidelights for social study. Many South Pacific cultures believe pregnancy comes from being splashed with sea water."

The women wade in calling the turtles.

Just what they say, he did not know. It probably was some ancient chant with magical properties.

In any case, turtles soon come popping up like bad debts.

They find the ocean full of chocolate cupcake. They swim to land and wind up fricassée.

I asked him if the lady turtle-callers had to stay

away from anything to prepare for this giant Diners' Club event.

Mr. Lane did not know exactly. He suspected it would be coconut. Coconut is tabu whenever you are pulling any magic or calling on the gods for cooperation.

In many islands of the South Pacific, women are forbidden certain kinds of fish. Mainly fish that have magical properties for men.

"It is well known that women steal a man's *mana*, his power. Therefore, they must not have anything to do with magic properties."

Something like taking their mink coat away. Only, of course, in this climate, you'd look silly calling turtles in mink.

Captain Trevor Withers will be buried with the ghosts of 87 virgins. This is a better deal than is put out by any Stateside mortuary and the Captain is very proud of it.

Captain Withers sails the yacht *Blue Lagoon* from Lautoka in the Fijis down to the remote Yasawa Islands. He carries 10 tourists on each trip. The charges are $100 each for everything for four days—including a ceremonial belt of kava.

"The natives are already preparing my grave three thousand feet up on that peak there," said the Captain. "That is where eighty-seven virgins jumped off to avoid an invading Tonga army. It is a very great honor."

Captain Withers has been sailing the dangerous reefs of the Yasawas since the end of World War II.

Passengers board at 10 in the morning. A mimeographed sheet of instructions is left under your door at the South Pacific Hotel the night before:

> You may already be aware that the *Blue Lagoon* differs in several more or less subtle respects from the *Queen Mary*. It is only 55 feet in length and space for storage of large suitcases is accordingly restricted.

What is best for baggage, said the Captain, is a two-pound bag of hard candy.

The Yasawa natives were cannibals. The way to handle a cannibal is to spoil his appetite by letting him eat candy before dinner—that is my idea.

The 87 virgins (said Captain Withers) were from the village of Yalobi.

The King of the Yasawas lives in Yalobi.

"Funny thing about the Tonga invasion," said Captain Withers. "The Tongans were really after pandanus mats. They make the best pandanus mats here. The women were just added booty."

The fame of pandanus mats from Yalobi was akin to the better mousetrap.

The Tonga islanders began beating a warpath to the door.

"The Tongans invaded these islands about three times a year. They're Polynesians, you know—the Yasawans are Melanesian, black with frizzy hair.

"Now every time they raided and ran off with the pandanus, the village girls would hike up that lava mountain and hide in a cave.

"The fact is the Tongans came so often, the girls had to hide so often, they actually wore a path up the side of the hill.

"The Tongans spotted the path.

"When the girls saw they were discovered, the King's wife jumped first. And the eighty-seven virgins followed. It's a rather dramatic story."

We sleep on deck on the *Blue Lagoon*. The Southern Cross rides high in the heaven and a warm trade wind blows through the rigging.

The white surf thunders on a crescent of silver sand. The coco palms are black-green on the shoreline and the mountain of the 87 virgins, rising above the still lagoon, is like a jagged cardboard cutout.

"The spirits of Kings walk along the beach at night," said Captain Withers. "Spirits are strong in the island.

"When they carry me up the peak, they will send me up with five hundred strong men. A ladder of men.

"They must be careful not to drop me. If they do, a little piece of me will drop off and become a devil which will haunt the village forever.

"Handle with care is the word."

The Captain looked as if he enjoyed the prospect.

One of the worst things you can do, if you are going skindiving, is run around with girls.

This is well known in the Yasawa Islands, four cruising days south of Lautoka in the Fijis. Since the snorkel-and-mask business is becoming more and more popular, this information ought to be passed on.

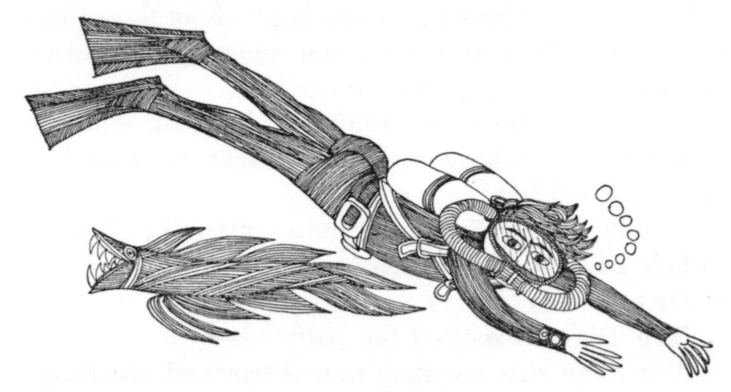

"When we go diving on the ocean reef, we have a ceremony first.

"We talk to the Shark-god. We throw tobacco on the water and kava root. Then my boys tell the Shark-god: 'We swim in your waters today. We carry spears. But we do not hurt your sharks. Spears for barracuda.' "

The *Blue Lagoon* cruise takes four days. During that time, Captain Withers tells a number of stories—they are quite polished and I have an idea he has been rubbing them up for some time.

I asked him if there were many sharks.

"Plenty," said the Captain. "Oh, plenty of sharks. Big six-foot tiger sharks. Slice a man in half so he'd hardly know it. That's one thing always reported by people who've been bitten by sharks. The bite is so clean they hardly feel it.

"Now about this boy Bill I was telling you about.

"He'd been around with the girls the night before we sailed and he begged me not to make him dive. Pearls we were after.

" 'If I dive, I die,' he said.

"I was newer in the islands then," said the Captain. I've become a good deal more open-minded since, let me tell you.

"Anyway, I wanted to punish that boy. I gave him every dirty job on deck. I put him to cleaning fish for one thing.

"He got quite a bit of fish blood on him. He was tracking it around the deck and I told him, 'Go wash your feet.' "

The *Blue Lagoon* rolled easily in the blue sea and a warm trade wind blew across the decks.

"Well, sir, this boy went over to the rail and swung his feet into the water.

"Then, by jove, a tiger shark about eighteen feet long turned thirty yards out. That shark dodged through three boys swimming toward the ship, swung past them like a destroyer cutting through a convoy!

"I swear he was doing twenty-five knots! Moving!

"The tiger headed straight for the boy's dangling feet and that black boy turned just about white.

"He jerked his feet up and that shark hit the ship like a torpedo! Really rocked it. *Bang!*

"Yes, sir, I believe it when these boys say they can talk with the Shark-god."

* * *

With all this sailing into the Yasawas—not even a stop for island copra vessels—Captain Withers has become famous. He is now a Fijian High Chief.

"The islands change your viewpoint," he said. "Why, a well-educated Fiji police official retired down here to a little island. No water on the place. But he told me, 'My father's devil told me.' Devil or spirit, it's the same thing here.

"Said his father's devil told him to dig by the lemon tree. I could hardly believe he'd put faith in such hogwash.

"We sail past the island tomorrow," said the Captain,

"and he'll come out and wave at us. I'd like you to pay particular attention to the stream of water by his hut. By the lemon tree."

The King of the Yasawas has gray hair that stands eight inches high like a wire brush. Don't touch his kava cup!

"Take pictures. Pass out candy to the kids. But for heaven's sake, don't touch the King's cup," said Captain Withers nervously.

The yacht *Blue Lagoon* has stopped for a ceremonial bowl of kava with the barefoot King.

"It is made from a root," said Captain Withers. "Non-alcoholic, but it's supposed to have a light drug in it of some sort. Anyway, some people say your tongue gets a little numb after a lot of it.

"The main thing is not to touch the King's cup. *Tabu.* Bad luck."

To enforce this restriction, the King is surrounded by a dozen big, black warriors with frizzy hair. They thump their spears on the ground and wear lampblack under the eyes to scare hell out of everybody.

The ceremony is conducted sitting down, in a circle. The kava root is powdered.

"In the old days, correctly, the kava root was chewed fresh and spat into the bowl. It should be chewed only by virgins," said Withers.

The kava root these decadent days is powdered—heaven only knows who chewed it.

You add water. Presto! Instant kava.

The King watched this process glumly.

The trade wind blew through the palm trees. Beyond the lagoon, the surf beat a thundering white line of foam on the reef.

The King's cupbearer filled the King's cup—*he* can touch it.

The warriors thumped their spears and began a chant.

You clap your hands once. The King's cupbearer pours a little kava into your half coconut shell. (Don't touch the cup!)

You bang this down—it's a little bland and bitter. Tastes a little like the stuff the dentist gives you to rinse your mouth.

Withers said he was looking for a partner in these Yasawas cruises. He wants to buy a New Zealand yacht that sleeps 18.

"A youngish chap who does some sailing," said Withers. "If he could play the ukulele, it'd be an advantage. He'd have to invest five thousand dollars. But if you like this life, it's a lifetime security."

On the *Blue Lagoon,* Withers doesn't serve kava. He serves dry martinis. You can touch any old cup you want to.

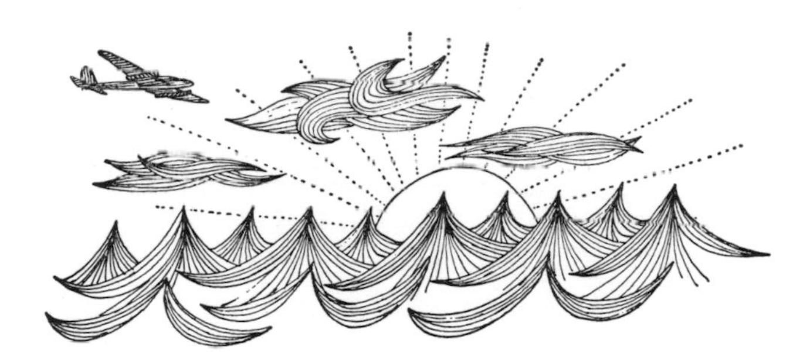

INDEX

About the Author

A Pulitzer Prize-winning journalist with twenty-five years of experience, and now traveling around the world somewhere for half of each year and writing about it for twelve million readers, Stan Delaplane is also the author of *Postcard from Delaplane* and *The Little World of Stanton Delaplane,* both best sellers, and *Delaplane in Mexico* (with Robert de Roos) and a collection of his famed columns, *And How She Grew.* He won the Pulitzer Prize for his 1942 coverage of a movement by six California and Oregon counties to secede and form a new state of Jefferson. He also has two National Headliners' Awards, one for his feature on "The Ding Dong Daddy of the D Car Line," and the second for consistently outstanding feature columns. In 1962 he was awarded the Pacific Area Travel Association (PATA) Award for the best series of articles on the Pacific, an award appropriately presented to him in Hong Kong.